D1095930

MAKING AND COLLECTING
MILITARY MINIATURES

Behind The Turnpike Fence

Battle of Sharpsburg — September 17th, 1862

The figures in this dramatic scene are the work of several American craftsmen and each figure was altered to interpret the particular action of the moment. The overall size of the diorama is fifteen by seventeen inches; the grass was made from hemp fiber cut one-eighth and one-quarter inches long and inserted in the moist scenic base; the groundwork was painted with Flo-Paque colors. Bits of thin metal, chain, wire and the like were used to add small details; fragments of battle litter, such as the canteen on the road, were cast of plaster. The diorama was built by William Alexander.

Photo by Robert Johnson

MAKING AND COLLECTING
MILITARY MINIATURES

by

BOB BARD

ROBERT M. McBRIDE CO., INC.
New York

First edition
Second Printing

Library of Congress Catalog
Card Number 57-10757

Printed in the United States of America

Published simultaneously in Canada by
Burns & MacEachern
Toronto

This book is dedicated to

THE YOUNG IN HEART.

Growing old is just a matter of losing interest and dying by degrees. Youth burns eternal in the breast of the creative and the curious; these are today's Hobbyists.

CONTENTS

Introduction

In centuries to come, archaeologists and historians may well refer to our time as the Hobby Age. Hobbies sooner or later enter into almost every conversation. Large corporations encourage their employees to band together in hobby groups; doctors recommend hobbies as an ally to their medicines and services; thousands of people with time on their hands find a fuller life through hobbies. Until recently, people with hobbies were looked upon as eccentric, but today, in most circles, if you can't offer tid-bits of conversation on some avocation or hobby, you don't belong.

Television and radio commentators and stars eagerly welcome hobbyists on their programs to talk about their avocations; columnists find hobbies a bright spark to liven their columns; national magazines devote many pages to hobbies and to the people who have them. Springing from natural instincts, hobbies have been indulged in since before written history. There is reason to believe that the cave man, in prehistoric days, passed away idle moments by drawing on the walls of his cave. Further along in history, when Matilda, the Queen of William the Conqueror, embroidered the famous and treasured Bayeux Tapestry, it is reasonable to assume that she was following her hobby of needlework. So it goes through the ages; people have always had hobbies. Museums throughout the world display many objects which are the handiwork of hobbyists centuries ago.

Today, hobbies have become an important part of everyday life, with thousands of converts made every month. Truly, this is the golden age of hobbies. Apostles and missionaries of hobbies pass through the land spreading the hobby gospel by word of mouth and the printed page. Each hobby has its joys, satisfactions, and other attractions; however, who can deny the innate fascination of the military uniform and the instinctive desire to create? Present-day society, with its added leisure time and its natural creative desires and military fascination, is without a doubt greatly responsible for the rising popularity of making and collecting military miniatures.

Naturally, Philistines in the land look down upon the hobbyist and question his mentality, referring to his miniatures as toys. The smug realist is right in his appraisal of the hobbyist's miniatures as toys, because toys are tools of play and relaxation. He greatly underestimates the mental capacity of the hobbyist, however, for the man who has learned that play and relaxation are just as important to his well being as the air he breathes and the food he eats is indeed a practical, intelligent person.

Knocking a little ball around a field with a club in an effort to get it into a hole isn't much different from shooting at miniature soldiers in a war game. Searching through books and prints, or going into the fields to find subjects to sketch or paint on canvas, certainly isn't different from searching through museums and libraries for uniform information to be reproduced in a miniature, or visiting a battle field in order to reproduce particular terrain in a diorama. No matter in what manner relaxation is found, be it a $5,000 sports car, tropical fish, golf, or bridge, the participants are playing with toys. The method of obtaining relaxation is very much like the old lady who kissed a cow, it's purely a matter of taste.

Making and collecting military miniatures as a leisure pursuit has much to recommend it. For those who like to mold, shape and carve, its possibilities are unlimited. For the artistically inclined who like to paint and create scenic effects, miniatures and dioramas offer ample scope for their abilities. And for those who just like things military and thrill to uniforms, parades and battles, duplicating in miniature the events of military history with commercially produced models can give hours of enjoyment.

Technical data and foreign terms which might confuse the novice have purposely been avoided in the writing of this book. Descriptions and instructions are written in terms that make the understanding of each project easy; after all a person pursues his hobby for the pleasure he derives from it and not for problems and difficulties. Each step, each plan and process has been thoroughly tried and tested to assure its success by anyone carefully following the instructions.

This book covers ground which no other book, to the best of our knowledge, has attempted. Much credit is due to many hobbyists for ideas and suggestions that have been incorporated in this volume, far too many to list in detail. A few are credited with illustrations and others through the text, but much material has been drawn from reams of correspondence, contact with hobbyists and actual practice.

A single figure, a group or even a diorama may be completed, but a military miniature collection is never finished because there is always some change or addition to be made, and this is one of the many things that make the hobby fascinating. When you discover the unlimited prospects of fun and relaxation that making and collecting military miniatures can offer, you too will become as enthusiastic as thousands of other collectors, including myself.

Baltimore, Maryland   B O B   B A R D
March 1, 1957

CHAPTER 1

Model Soldiers

Making and collecting military miniatures is certainly nothing new. From time immemorial, man has created images of his heroes and gods. Since wars and rumors of war have been man's heritage, it is only natural to find the craftsman, both amateur and professional, making images that wear the uniforms and armor of the fighting man.

Be they toys, scale models, works of art, military training aids or just dust catchers, these small reproductions of soldiers and machines of war have fascinated people around the globe for thousands of years. Just as the history of man is filled with both fact and fancy, the narrative of the little soldiers made from base and precious metals, terra cotta, wood and other materials, must also contain not only proven facts, but legends and suppositions of the scholars as well. In museum collections throughout the world, especially in France, England and Germany, there are examples of small military figures from the very early ages of man up to those of modern craftsmen. All the modern figures and most of those from the middle ages on are well documented, and there is no

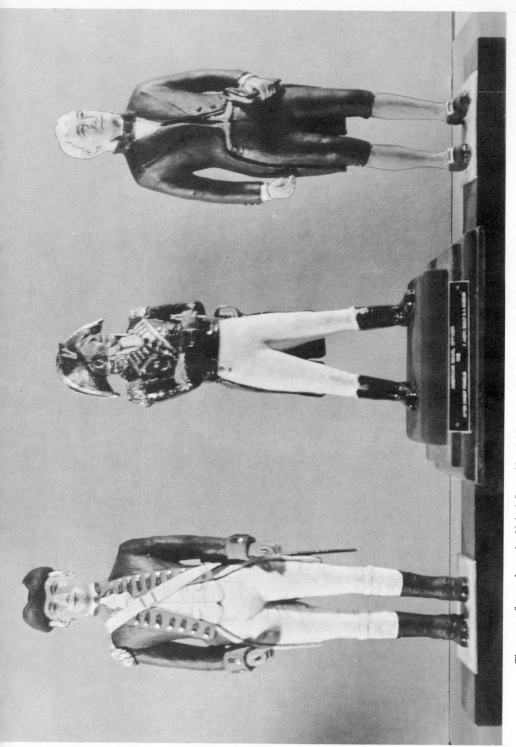

Three wax figures from the United States Naval Museum in Annapolis, from left to right; Marine officer 1776, United States Navy officer 1812 and United States Navy chaplain 1830. The tallest figure in the group is eleven and three quarter inches high.

Napoleon and the Old Guard by Metayer of France, on display in the West Point Museum.

question about their original purpose. However, although the very ancient examples are military miniatures or model soldiers, there is no definite proof of their precise purpose. From the tombs of the Ancient Egyptians, there are little wooden foot soldiers bearing spears, and also charioteers. In Sardinia and Italy, archaeologists have unearthed small bronze figures wearing helmets and carrying the small shield and short sword of the Phoenician warrior. Ancient grave mounds in many countries have yielded cavalrymen, foot troops and war chariots of various materials, even mixtures of tin and lead. A mounted figure of Caesar, unearthed at Pesaro in Italy, along with castings of Roman legionaires made of lead and tin mixtures found at Mainz, certainly confirms that the Romans were familiar with the little lead soldier.

Since many of the early examples mentioned were obtained from tombs and burial mounds, it is natural to assume that the miniatures were not intended to be toys. Ancient burial rites often provided for the deceased's protection and comfort in the next world by entombing with him servants, food and guards, along with other necessities of life, according to his wealth and rank. In some cases, actual people were killed and buried with their masters; however in most burials, models of the personnel and equipment needed for the deceased's comfort on his journey were placed in the tomb with him. Considering that other items not of a military nature were also found

3

Both the Harles and the Wirths are husband-and-wife teams who share their hobby of making and collecting military miniatures. The two historical dioramas, featured in the permanent Marine Corps exhibit at the National Museum of the Smithsonian Institution, are being presented to General Lemuel C. Shepherd, Jr., by the donors, Mr. and Mrs. John C. Wirth (exhibit on the left) and Mr. and Mrs. William G. Harle (exhibit on the right).

when unearthing many of the miniature soldiers mentioned, the logical assumption is that they were actually religious symbols. Although this may indicate that in the ancient world a man had to die in order to collect military miniatures, simple deduction would suggest this was not true, and that toy soldiers were most likely a familiar object in the lives of the ancients.

The basic desires, needs and passions of man have not changed through the ages. The methods and speed of accomplishing the eventual end have changed, but the ancient's pride of possession, the spirit of conquest, the need for shelter, food and relaxation or play were just as strong as today. Children of the prehistoric and ancient world admired heroes just as much as modern children do, and there is no question that boys of those bygone ages fought many a mock battle with wooden swords and shields. It is also logical to believe that fathers, uncles or maybe the metal worker in the hut down the way made model armies for the boys' amusement. They may have been of wood, clay or even cast from metal, because man was well advanced in the art of casting many centuries before the birth of Christ. And men, being men, no doubt joined in the play, setting the miniatures out in formations, showing their sons how dad won the last war almost single handed. In the homes of the Romans there could have been a model of the Trojan horse with Homeric warriors that could be placed inside. This is supposition, of course, for the ravages of time and the enthusiasm of a boy's miniature battles do not lend themselves to preserving historic relics. How many adult collectors today can find the leaden armies they shot down in childhood.

There is no question that miniature soldiers were a popular form of amusement during the middle ages and were made to be played with, since a number of old wood cuts show young people with them. One particularly interesting wood cut by Hans Burgkmair — who did a series of plates showing the activities of Emperor Maximilian I — shows him as a child playing with a pair of

5

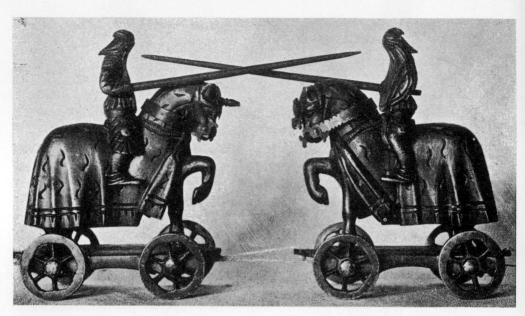

These bronze figures of jousters, made during the fifteenth century, are designed to run against each other by means of pulleys, unseating one of the knights from his mount.

mounted knights which, by an ingenious system of wheels and strings, charged each other in a realistic manner and splintered their lances which were made of brittle wood. It is also recorded that Maximilian presented a set of jousting knights mounted on wooden horses to young King Louis II of Hungary. A number of small lead and tin figures of knights which were finished only on one side have been recovered from the Seine, and are supposed to have been made during the thirteenth century or earlier. However, since the figures found resemble particular persons such as Saint George and others, they may have been a type of insignia or badge rather than toys, but the final answer is still open to debate.

Mechanical toys were well known in the sixteenth century, and in the latter part of that century Daniel Bertel of Lubeck, Germany, offered, beside mechanical figures that could walk, dance and do acrobatics, a fleet of galleys with Turks and Christians engaged in battle at sea. Historic records indicate that little soldiers were a standard toy of royal children. Louis III had a set of miniature soldiers that fitted into holes of a flat board and Louis XIV had in his youth an army of miniature soldiers made of silver which are reputed to have cost 50,000 thalers. As a youth, Louis XV possessed an even more elaborate set of silver soldiers. It is said that the minister of war, Marquis de Vauban, journeyed to Nuremberg to oversee the creation of the set by the celebrated craftsman Hans Hautch and his son Gottfried. This set of miniatures was so cleverly made that ingenious mechanical devices allowed the operator to put the soldiers through the various drills of the day. Unfortunately, the little tin and lead figures of the dauphins did not survive, and the silver ones were melted down to help fill the French treasury during lean years. However, letters and records preserved in various museums give authenticity to their existence and operation.

Museums also preserve examples of less elaborate miniatures made during this and other periods, some of crude workmanship and others of intricate detail. Models of knights in full detailed armor are in some cases so fine that it raises the question as to whether they were actually toys or models for armor. But documents prove that such detailed creations were made to be given as gifts and to be played with. Considering the many types preserved in museum and private collections from these earlier centuries, common logic would suggest that playing with miniature soldiers was one of the leading pastimes of the day; those figures of the middle class and peasants not as fine as those of nobility, but none the less brave when maneuvered over imaginary battle fields by their young commanders.

The few modern hobbyists who assume an attitude of hurt pride when their collections are compared with toys, will no doubt be pleased to learn that during the seventeenth and eighteenth centuries the term had a much broader meaning. The word "Toy" was not used only to designate children's playthings, but also referred to any small article. Within the various guilds there were

7

1802

1814

1825

1837

1840

1875

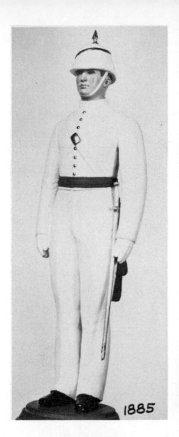

1885

1899

1920

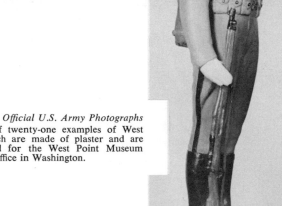

1930

Ten plaster figures from the collection of twenty-one examples of West Point Cadet uniforms. These figures, which are made of plaster and are about fourteen inches tall, were designed for the West Point Museum collection by the Quartermaster General's Office in Washington.

craftsmen who did not consider it beneath their dignity to make miniatures or models of larger pieces for their patrons; neither did they refuse commissions from wealthy customers for miniatures of soldiers and other military pieces. Needless to say, models created by these artists were, in most cases, of superb workmanship and are generally the miniatures that are found preserved in museum collections.

Frederick the Great, who fought all the great powers of Europe, and the soldier whom all other soldiers of Europe tried to imitate, was in a way responsible for miniature soldiers reaching the stage of large production for the masses. The exploits of Frederick were told and retold throughout the world and the people were very military conscious. Taking advantage of this military fervor, Andreas Hilpert of Coburg in 1760 started the mass production of miniature soldiers and is, without a doubt, the originator of the toy soldiers as we know them today. Mass production made the little soldiers a familiar figure in play rooms throughout the world and the armies of different countries dressed in proper uniforms were added as fast as possible, for no country was content until the Hilperts made models of its soldiers. The Hilpert soldiers were made of tin and engraved on both sides and stood on flat bases like the "Flats" of today. Personalities, such as Frederick, his generals and other famous people, were made a little larger than the other figures, and more care was taken in their painting. Many examples of these soldiers exist today in museums and private collections; there are catalogs which were published by the Hilperts still in existence showing the great varieties of miniatures they produced, including wild and domestic animals, scenic items and civilians as well as soldiers. "Get a good thing going and imitators will spring up like mushrooms" was just as true in the eighteenth century as it is today, and by the end of the seventeen hundreds there were many makers of tin soldiers on a mass production basis. Most of the casting and painting was done on a piece work basis in homes, after the forms or molds had been

10

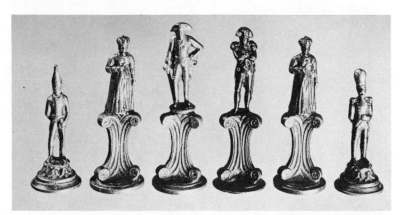

Photograph by Johnson

Iron chess pieces made in Germany during the nineteenth century. These are well detailed castings of Frederick the Great and Napoleon, each with his Queen and grenadier officers serving as bishops in the set. Allegedly these figures were cast from metal taken from captured British cannon. A complete set is shown in the chapter on war games.

engraved. Tin and lead were used for casting and there was no standard height or scale for the figures; they varied from 30 to 60 mm. tall and even larger.

The exploits of Frederick followed by the wars of Napoleon made the miniature soldiers even more popular, not only as toys but to instruct soldiers in the art of war. Little tin soldiers became standard visual aids in instructing young officers to maneuver troops and are still used for that purpose. Fortunately, several of the manufacturers got together and decided on a standard height for figures so that armies of greater variety could be assembled; the size decided on was 30 to 32 mm. for foot figures with all other figures and equipment conforming in scale. Most "Flats" of today are still made to this standard.

With the exception of special pieces the painting and finishing on most of the soldiers wasn't good, since the painters often knew little if anything about uniforms. In the natural course of events, collectors removed the original paint and repainted the figures in proper colors. As the practice, or hobby, of repainting spread, the alert

Toy lead figures which were popular in the very early part of the twentieth century. These might be termed semi-flat because they were not really flat or full round, as shown by the figure turned sideways at the back of the group. The figures in this group were cast on the horse and could not be removed.

German makers started to turn out unpainted castings which the hobbyist could finish himself. Figures also started to appear on the market with engraving of higher relief, in what might be called semi-flat, and eventually fuller-bodied figures were made until they blossomed forth full-around as usually seen in stores today. However, this doesn't mean the little "Flats" are gone, they are still made and still popular, not only with collectors, but for training service as in the days of Frederick and Napoleon.

The early three-dimension figures were in most cases cast in stiff unnatural poses and like the earlier "Flats" were painted in haphazard fashion. Collectors desiring more life-like action started to remove paint and cut arms and legs off, soldering them in more natural positions and then painting in authentic colors. People of like interests seek each other and eventually during the first half of the twentieth century, military miniature clubs were formed where collectors could trade information and figures. Just as the little soldiers' popularity grew until they are being manufactured in almost every country

12

on the face of the globe, so the hobby of making and collecting military miniatures spread until it is a universal pastime today, enjoyed by men, women and children from all walks of life.

The military miniature collector is not an antique collector; his interest is in the authenticity of uniforms and equipment in his miniature collection, and not in how long ago the figures were made. Today there are skilled craftsmen turning out superb lead figures in accurate detail that are truly works of art, and collectors with sufficient hobby budgets make collections of these little masterpieces, and often commission the artists to create particular models. There are also miniature makers who create detailed castings of figures in life-like poses and correct uniforms which the collector with a smaller budget, or because he enjoys painting, can assemble and paint in the proper colors. Most of these skilled makers are former hobbyists who started making miniature soldiers for themselves, when they could not find commercial figures to their exacting tastes, and found

One of the early types of "full round" lead soldiers distributed by Mc-Loughlin Brothers of New York. The standing figures are about two inches tall; the mounted figure is cast separately, and can be removed from the horse.

Another group of very early twentieth century lead soldiers which are neither flat nor full-round, as is indicated by the last figure in the group. The mounted figure can be removed from his horse. The designer of this early set was a little careless with scale since the foot figures, which are about two inches tall, are almost as tall as the mounted one.

there were other collectors eager to buy their creations.

One type of collector finds his greatest joy in searching for toy soldiers which he can convert into collectors' pieces by changing and adding details such as properly colored insignia and uniforms. Probably the most envied collectors are those who not only do the research, but also create the original model, make the mold, cast the figure and paint the soldier.

The majority of today's collections are made up of the three dimension or full round figures. There are several good reasons for this preference. They are the most life-like, for they have height, width and depth so that they may be viewed from any angle. There are more manufacturers of the full round figures and most of the manufacturers conform to a standard size, foot figures 54 to 55 mm. tall (about 2⅛ inches) and other figures in proportion; this gives the collector a great variety to select from. The same scale is found in both the mass-produced inexpensive figures and in the better figures; so the hobbyist can convert the very inexpensive figures to more accurate models by replacing arms, heads, etc., which have been taken from other figures, bought separately or made by the collector himself. The full round

14

Tamerlane, Napoleon (at the time of his Egyptian campaign), Henry VIII and Antoine Collinet (Count de La Salle) one of Napoleon's cavalry generals. These figures are standard height metal castings two and one eighth inches high.

Modern flats of French infantrymen from the World War I period. Although only about as thick as a dime notice how the deep engraving gives the figures depth. Also noteworthy is their realistic action which is one of the outstanding qualities of flats. Flats usually are sold in sets of about fifteen to eighteen figures in a number of action poses; one firm alone lists almost 700 different sets, from ancients to moderns.

figure also permits the addition of flowing capes, packs and other fine details which would not be possible on anything but three dimension figures.

Next in popularity are the famous "Flats" which are still being produced in the same scale set so many years ago by the early soldier makers. Flats are the real "Tin Soldier" of song and story, and are as their name indicates — flat — just about as thick as a dime. They are cast generally from tin and lead and the details, which in most cases are exceptionally good, stand out in high relief like the designs on a coin. The variety of figures and positions obtainable seems almost unlimited, ranging from ancient to modern. Just as these figures served in training for Napoleon's men, they also served in recent wars, and you will find modern soldiers in a variety of action poses with modern weapons. Flats lend themselves well to making shadow boxes and dioramas, which are viewed directly from the front. When seen in this manner they are very effective, because the relief detail and usually good painting give the illusion of depth. The compactness of Flats is also an advantage, since their smaller

16

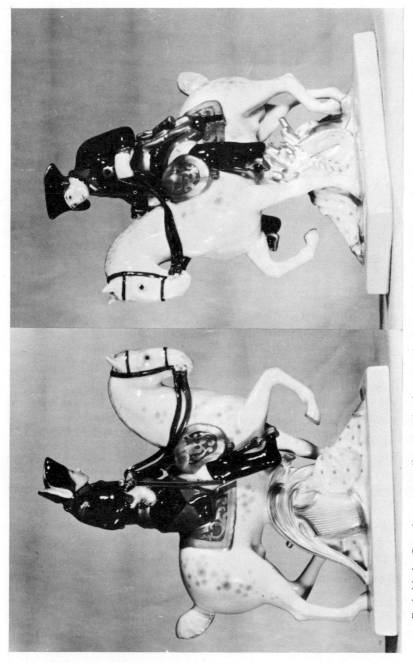

Frederick the Great in an outstanding example of a porcelain character piece. Frederick was far from a well man during the latter years of his life; the artist, as will be seen, has caught the feeling of pain in expression and position of the figures. Worthy of note is the cane hanging from the figure's right hand. The overall height of these pieces is six inches.

A very distinctive group of wooden soldiers. These little fellows, made in Germany, are only one inch tall, neatly painted in full color, and are mounted on a block of wood two-by-five inches.

size requires less space per figure, and storage space is naturally less for the war game enthusiast if he must pack his warriors away after each battle.

Although much of the foregoing has dealt with tin, lead and the more elaborate silver toy figures, this does not mean no miniatures or figurines of soldiers were made from other materials. Military figures were produced in porcelain that were superb in detail and authenticity of uniform and bore the marks of world renowned makers. Potteries of Europe still make many porcelain military figurines, some being cast in the original molds of many years ago. Ceramic military figurines have also been made, and there are hobbyists who, in addition to collecting military miniatures, make ceramics and porcelains that are exceptionally fine pieces even in the small 54 mm. size.

Wood has always been a favorite medium for many artisans and many such figures have been made through the centuries, some crude and some with intricate detail. Both toys and works of art have been produced in wood, and even today there are many fine military miniatures or figurines being carved from wood. An outstanding example of fine wooden figures are those depicting the Scottish uniforms, made by Pilkington-Jackson and on display at the Naval and Military Museum in Edinburgh.

18

Above, a Highland chief of 1660; below, a Highland piper of 1714. These superb figures were carved from Scottish oak by Pilkington Jackson. Each figure is about eighteen inches tall and painted in life-colors but in such a manner that the grain of the wood is not concealed. The figures are historically accurate and realistic down to the last button and check on the tartan; they will satisfy the military and costume experts, and they have vitality, solidity and all the virtue of perfectly "free" sculpture.

Figures made by Charles Sandre, believed to have been a senior officer of Napoleon's army, and made while in prison at Dartmoor before Waterloo. The bodies of the figures are made of wood, the clothing and equipment in cloth, metal, leather and fur in exact duplication of full-size military uniforms and equipment. The material in dressing the figures is

Wood has also been used in making models of various machines of war and military wagons. Wooden figures have also been clothed with real cloth, leather and metal, having all the clothing and equipment in exact detail, even down to the embossing on the tiny buttons. Even mixtures of wood pulp have been cast around wire armatures to make miniature soldiers.

Probably one of the oldest types of soldiers that are still being made are those of cardboard. These are to be found, both hand painted and printed, and in a variety of sizes. Cardboard cut-out soldiers are usually referred to as "Alsatian Soldiers" because for many years the making of cardboard soldiers was a specialty of Alsace. It is recorded that Louis XV played with a set of cardboard soldiers, consisting of infantry and cavalry, that

believed to be from pieces of uniforms given to Sandre by fellow prisoners. Even the small buttons, less than one-sixteenth inch in diameter, are fully embossed in detail with the Napoleonic eagle.

The figures are fourteen and one-half inches tall not including headgear and base. To the right of each figure is a standard 54mm lead figure and to the left a 30mm flat. From left to right are shown; Sapeur of the grenadiers, lancer and a fusilier grenadier.

were made by Henri de Gissey, designer of the Royal Ballet. The true Alsatian soldier is about five inches high and set in a wooden block for a base. Other cardboard soldiers are printed on sheets to be cut out, and they are even to be found in the form of cigarette and candy inserts.

There have been plastic figures for some years, but needless to say, the great boom in plastics of recent years has brought floods of plastic soldiers on the market, and they can be found on toy counters throughout the world. Like the items made of other materials, some are crude and others rival the finest examples made of metal. They are made not only in finished miniatures, but also in kits from which the hobbyist may assemble and paint his own figures. How much favor plastics will gain with

21

Paper cutout soldiers come in many ways and are made for advertising and for sale to collectors. This sheet contains figures in full color; the largest standing figures measure about four inches tall without headgear. On the back is the name of each figure and small paper easels permit the figures to stand up.

the old dyed-in-the-wool collector is yet to be seen, but the quality of workmanship and detail in many is certainly worthy of note. Some of the old timers, even though they do not wholly approve of plastics, still use them as models in making figures of metal, and this in itself is the most sincere compliment that could be paid to the plastic figures, even if they don't have the heft of metal.

The heritage of the miniature soldier is a long and noble one and his popularity and esteem grows with each succeeding year. More and more he appears in world-famous museums to recreate scenes from history and events of today. School children are deeply impressed by small figures moved about on miniature stages and sand tables, recreating events of history, and they absorb their lessons more quickly because it's fun to learn from three-dimensional miniatures. Military school instructors are turning everyday to miniatures as aids in instructing cadets in the arts of war, because tactics are understood more easily when students can see and move troops and equipment. Military commanders encourage their troops to become military miniature hobbyists, because miniature collecting leads to historic research and eventually, in many cases, to the study of military tactics. And thousands of people are making and collecting military miniatures as a form of relaxation.

Only a bold and ambitious person indeed would attempt to set down a chronological, minutely-detailed history of model soldiers, listing their types and makers along with all the famous collectors of the past and pres-

Cigarette card cutouts. These little figures are printed on cardboard and provided with a section at the bottom to form an easel. The name of the soldier is printed on the reverse side. Many years ago cutouts such as these were placed in packages of cigarettes, chocolate and other articles. (Other insert cards are found in the chapter on source material.)

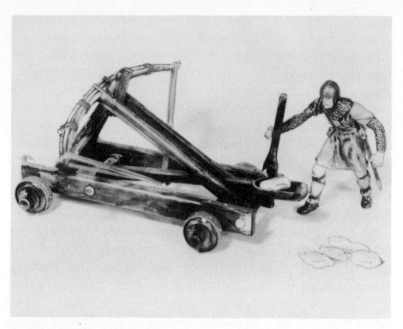

A fully operating catapult in a plastic model made in Germany. It is exceptionally well detailed and will throw an actual stone about ten feet. Plastic figures, such as the one about to fire the catapult, are also made in a variety of poses.

ent. Accurate records can be found on many collectors and manufacturers, but there have been hundreds of makers whose production was small and in many cases known only in their local areas. Even today new makers come on the scene periodically, some to be recognized only in their immediate locality, others to gain international fame among collectors for a few years or even months and then to pass out of the picture, while still others remain constant on the scene and their names become synonymous with the types of figures they produce. No longer does Europe monopolize the miniature soldier field in manufacturing or collecting, for today military miniatures are made and collected all over the globe, with the United States fast becoming a leader in the production of inexpensive, medium class and finely detailed models that rival the figures made by the best artisans of the old world.

One of Hannibal's war elephants. The figures are about two inches tall with the elephant in scale. The arms of the figures may be bent to various positions.

Ladies of the Court. The fair sex who enjoy a definite place in military miniature collections — princesses, queens and mistresses, as well as military leaders such as Joan of Arc — have been created in miniature. Dioramas have been built depicting slave markets, victory marches and battle scenes in which women are an important part.

No attempt has been made here to write a complete history of so vast a subject, but rather just an outline recalling episodes in the widespread story of model soldiers. Details of types and lengthy lists of statistics have been purposely avoided, because the military miniature collector does not base the value of his collection on rarity as collectors of stamps, coins, and antiques do, but on perfection of detail, workmanship and authenticity of uniforms and equipment. The true military miniature collector cares nothing about the age of a figure, for he is primarily a lover of books and research, deciding for himself what figures from what period interest him and, if such models do not exist, he converts another figure, creates a figure himself, or commissions someone to make it for him.

CHAPTER **2**

Collecting Military Miniatures

There is more truth than poetry in the popular song, "There is Something About a Soldier that is Grand, Grand, Grand," and who can deny the fascination of miniature models. The combination of these two inherent characteristics in most people accounts in no small way for the ever increasing number who turn to the making and collecting of military miniatures as a hobby.

Modern living conditions have made possible many more hours for relaxation and play, but offices and factories are filled with frustrated artists, sculptors, and historians who have been caught in the web of earning a living in the work-a-day world, rather than following their desires. Increasing pressure built up day after day from constant monotonous work must have a release or something is going to blow up. A hobby is the perfect safety valve for such pent up emotion because the hobbyist creates a world all his own where worries and problems are shut out; the few hours spent in pursuing his avocation release pressures and give him a clearer head and more relaxed nerves to tackle again the problems of earning a living.

27

Photo by Johnson

Making and collecting military miniatures is an excellent Father and Son hobby. John Barnes and his son Mike, derive many hours of fun and companionship through their hobby.

Before and after painting. A great variety of castings which depict various soldiers can be purchased from dealers in military miniatures. These castings usually are made with arms and equipment separate for fastening in the position desired by the hobbyist. The examples shown here are two figures assembled ready for painting and after being painted. The painting was the work of William Driscoll.

Making and collecting military miniatures has much to offer as a hobby because it incorporates history, geography and biography along with an opportunity to use one's hands. Smoldering in the breast of almost every human being is a desire to create things with his hands, and no hobby can afford greater opportunity to fulfill this desire. Unlike most creative hobbies, the collecting of military miniatures does not require any specific amount of space to accommodate its activities. Making and collecting military miniatures can be enjoyed just as much in a boarding house room as it can in the most spacious mansion. Individual figures or small groups can be blended into the decor of any room and are welcomed spots of color and interest.

A group of military figures in porcelain, which for centuries has been a medium for making figurines. Old pieces may be found in antique shops. Modern porcelain manufacturers are making military figures, some of them being cast from old molds. Porcelain produces a delicacy in both material and color which can't be duplicated in any other medium.

Although much of this book is devoted to the making of military miniatures, there is a great deal to be said for the pure collector who assembles collections of antique miniatures and the finished models of the professional figure maker. Old figures are still to be found in attics, second hand stores and antique shops. Where they are found and how much the owner thinks you want them, will have much to do with the value placed on them. On rare occasions, sets of old lead soldiers have been found in the general stores of small out-of-the-way towns, but needless to say, this is becoming rarer every day. But when it does happen, there is much gloating by both parties; the store keeper tells his cronies how he hung an item on a city slicker, and the collector beams as he exhibits his find to envious hobbyists, explaining how he bought them for less than the original list price.

Antique porcelain figures of soldiers, military suits of armor, wood carvings and many other items of interest to the military collector can still be found in antique stores and in the shops of dealers in art objects, arms and related subjects. Material of this type has a more or less set value, and if the shopkeeper is known to be reputable you may depend on his asking price. Auction sales on occasion include figures of this type and now and then some lead soldiers.

Collectors of antique model soldiers make up only a very small portion of the military miniature collecting fraternity, because the collector is generally more inter-

A Civil War artillery team galloping into action. This unusually life-like group was designed by Ralph G. Bussler. Displayed below are all the castings used to make it. As will be seen the horses are cast in two halves and the riders cast with arms separate. All of these parts are keyed and can easily be assembled with solder and cement.

Leon Chodnicki and a few of the many thousands of military miniatures which he has collected over a period of many years. Mr. Chodnicki's collection includes both antique and modern items of almost every type and material, and nearly every maker's work is represented in this vast collection. In addition to the work of others, his collection includes many fine dioramas and figures that he has made and painted himself.

In this top of a sectional bookcase used for display, cans are employed to raise figures in the back which would otherwise be obscured by those in front. The decoration across the back is made up of regimental cap badges although other types of background material may be used in the form of prints, draperies, medals and the like.

ested in authenticity and workmanship than he is in age. The collector is also a historian and usually is interested in one period or in the soldiers of one country. To set out to collect the soldiers of all countries would prove a monumental task, involving considerable problems in housing and financing. Hence, most collectors follow one of these methods in building his collection. First, he may buy from miniature or hobby dealers the finished models of the period that interests him. These are available in very fine detailed models and also in inexpensive sets. Second, he may search out the details in his own or the public library and commission a professional to create the model for him. Third, he may buy figures that are similar to the uniforms he desires and convert them to his particular interest. Fourth, he may purchase from his miniature or hobby dealer unfinished castings of a great number of periods and countries which he may assemble and paint. Finally, he can create the original figure himself.

Regardless of the type of figures collected, one of the greatest joys of the hobby is showing them off and there are many pleasing methods of doing this no matter how much or how little space is available. The miniature collector, being by nature a bibliophile, will have book cases or shelves about the room, and these are excellent

33

A shadow box with a mirror back can easily be made with an ordinary picture frame, a few pieces of wood and a mirror. The mirror adds greatly to the display because both the front and back of the figures may be seen at the same time.

places to display small dioramas or individual figures.

Sectional bookcases having glass doors are exceptionally good for display, because one or more sections can be devoted to miniatures, while the other sections can house books and reference material. Sectional cases also have the advantage of growing with your collection and the glass doors protect your miniatures and books. Decorative material may be draped or tacked around the back and sides of the section and individual figures displayed, or the section may be set up as a small stage with painted backdrop and scenery and an action group of figures. Interior lighting of the display section can be accomplished very easily and inexpensively, adding a great deal to the overall effect.

China closets, hanging curio cabinets, what-not shelves, breakfronts and many other types of furniture may be used to display miniatures and can be found at most furniture stores. Should the purchase of special cabinets place too much strain on the hobbyist's budget, there is always his ingenuity to fall back upon and the inventiveness of many collectors has produced very exciting methods of display.

Probably the simplest display case is the open front shadow box. These may be purchased at many furniture stores or the collector may make his own with very little effort. The back may be mirrored or plain; the mirror, however, adds little cost, and being able to see both the back and front of figures without touching them adds greatly to the charm of the display. To make a mirrored shadow box you will need a mirror, a picture frame and some wood ⅛ to ¼ inch thick and about 2½ inches wide. Buy a framed mirror and a picture frame that are the same size; these may be purchased at department stores, picture stores or the local ten-cent store. With the wood, build a box with the mirror as the bottom or back. The picture frame, without the glass,

This effective wall arrangement was made by using a mirrored shadow box and several small framed military prints.

is then put on the front of the box to trim it. Depending on the size of box you make, you may add one or two shelves inside the box from the wood. Place two strong rings or hangers on the back of the box; be sure they are even so that the box will hang level. Strategically placed shadow boxes of this type will add charm to any room and the selection of frame types will have much to do in matching modern or period room furnishings.

Hanging wall cases with glass fronts can be made in a great variety of sizes; in fact, the open front shadow box is converted into a glass front wall case by just placing plain glass tightly in the picture frame and hinging the frame to the box instead of fastening it permanently. One collector of flats, whose collection far exceeds his display space, has designed an ingenious wall case which permits him to change displays frequently and easily so that he can enjoy all his miniatures. The case can be built from wood ¾ to 1 inch thick and 3 to 4 inches wide and a practical size case is about 24 inches tall and 12 inches wide inside. After the side and end pieces are cut, slots are cut into the upright pieces to accommodate the shelves. These slots should be about 3 inches apart and perfectly level and straight so that the shelves will slide in and out easily. Assemble the ends and sides with screws, or nails and glue, making a back from plywood or any other sturdy material. The front is made from a picture frame of proper size with the glass firmly in place, the frame may be permanently hinged to the top of the box or hooks and eye bolts may be used so that the front may be lifted entirely off the box. Shelves are then cut of proper width and length to slide into the slots cut in the sides. Dioramas are then set up on the shelves and slid into the case.

Three dimensional pictures are always fascinating and decorative, and military miniatures lend themselves admirably to this type of display. The difference between shadow boxes and three dimensional pictures is that displays may be changed in the shadow box, but in the picture the display is set up permanently and sealed in

36

A wall case incorporating a box and a picture frame designed by Fredrick T. Wehr. The slotted sides permit the removal of the shelves on which to set up displays.

Haslet's Delaware Regiment leaving the Dover Green, Revolutionary War.

Photo by duVal

This diorama of Haslet's Delaware Regiment setting out from the Dover Green in the American Revolution, was made by Harry Barker. Built into a large shadow box this display is designed to be hung as a picture. The civilian figures in the background add life-like realism to the scene.

the frame. In the shadow box, no effort usually is made to tell a story; in the three dimensional picture, however, the figures are surrounded with props and scenery and placed in such a manner that they depict a particular event or scene. The background, or backdrop, may be painted by the collector, or a suitable picture may be found in a magazine. The important thing, in either painting or selecting a background picture, is to be sure the scene follows through in proper perspective with the foreground scenery and figures as explained in the chapter on "Dioramas and Scenery."

The bottom or floor of the rural or battleground scene should not meet the background directly, because the illusion of depth will be lost. This point where actual depth meets the illusion of depth should be camouflaged with shrubbery or a wall of some other scenery. In the case of a street scene, where buildings are involved, the structures may be painted flat on the backdrop and additional depth added by building balconies, steps, or window frames out from the painting. The high relief of the added detail will blend the three dimensions of the front into the two dimensions of the back with realistic effect. With proper planning and strict adherence to the rules of perspective, entire buildings may be built out from the background. By following carefully the angles to the vanishing points and skillfully decreasing the depth of color and distinctiveness of detail in the background, a most life-like scene can be created.

To avoid sharp corners at the top, the background may curve into the sky which is painted on the inside top of the frame box. Sharp corners at the sides may either be covered with scenic materials or the sides of the background may be curved into the sides of the frame. The most effective pictures are made by depicting the story with as few figures as possible, because a great clutter of figures will only add confusion and many times lose the point of the story being told.

The frames to house three-dimension pictures may be constructed the same as shadow boxes; then seal the

An unusual and practical display method, designed by E. L. Denniston, the basis of which is a piece of pegboard cut four by six feet and painted white. Small shelves are artistically arranged to display groups of figures and the remainder of the board is used to show framed prints and some of Mr. Denniston's war trophies. One of the great advantages of this display is that the format may be changed at will because of the flexibility of shelf-arrangement on pegboard.

decorative frame and glass permanently when the scene is completed. Effective 3-D pictures can also be made by selecting a frame with a very deep molding and building the little diorama within what would normally surround the picture. This is done by attaching a cover of plywood or other material across what would normally be the front edge of the deep frame; the figures and background are then placed within the box and the glass sealed in place upon completion. Frame boxes may also be made by placing two deep frames together in order to gain depth. These may be frames of the same type molding, or interesting and decorative effects may be obtained by combining molds of different types.

The military miniature collector, being by nature a

lover of military history, naturally has a love for maps. Many collectors gain their greatest delight in tracing and mentally refighting decisive campaigns on maps while admiring their military miniature collections. Some collectors combine these two interests by framing colorful campaign maps, which they have purchased or made themselves, in deep frames such as those used in three dimension pictures. The map forms the backdrop and the figures in front depict a particular incident of the campaign, or in some cases the figures signify the opposing leaders in the particular campaign mapped.

One well known collector of miniatures and scenes from military history has devised an unusual and decorative method of displaying not only items from his hobby but his personal war decorations as well. Using a piece of pegboard, which may be purchased from any lumber dealer, the hobbyist created a color spot that would be the envy of any interior decorator. The pegboard, measuring four by six feet, was carefully sanded and then painted to blend into the decor of the room where it appears. The outstanding feature of the pegboard is its adaptability to change. With little effort and no damage to the surface, the small wire pegs which hold the shelves may be fitted into any of the many holes in the board. The board was hung on the wall behind a server and small shelves were placed in a carefully thought out pattern on the board. Individual figures and small groups of military miniatures were placed on these shelves. The balance of the board is devoted to framed military prints, medals and other trophies collected during years in the service. This type of display never becomes monotonous, because re-arrangement can be made at any time. Experimenting with various arrangements adds a great deal of pleasure to the collector's hobby.

Methods and effects in displaying military miniatures are unlimited and depend upon the imagination of the collector. Displays worked into the bases of lamps and on bookends or on valances over windows and doors, are only a few of the many ingenious methods used by enthusiasts and decorators. Tasteful and effective display need not be hampered by a low budget, because the collector may build or convert many inexpensive materials into shelves, cases and display props.

For example, ordinary small boxes, such as cigar boxes, may be transformed into interesting display shelves by cementing or nailing several together and then painting or covering them with decorative material. The boxes may be arranged in any number of patterns to be hung on the wall or they may be fastened permanently and painted the color of the walls. Even light easily-worked wood such as balsa, which may be obtained in any model shop in a great variety of sizes, can be used to make satisfactory boxes and shelves for display.

Collectors who are not budget conscious may call upon carpenters and cabinet makers to create display cases for their collections. Some collectors have had even libraries, hobby rooms and club cellars built around their collections, with specially lighted cases built into the walls. Many professional men who are collectors bring a spot of color and interest into their offices with small shadow boxes or lamps displaying miniature soldiers. The love for soldiers and miniatures is no respecter of social or financial position. It is one of the few hobbies so wide in scope and flexible in application that everyone may enjoy collecting military miniatures, no matter what his station in life.

To exhibit small groups or types in cabinets, it is necessary, in order to obtain the best display value, to use display props to raise figures in the rear above those in the foreground. This may be done by building sets of steps from wood or cardboard and finishing in harmonious colors. A very pleasing and rich effect may also be obtained by placing a variety of small boxes in strategic spots in the case and then draping cloth over the boxes and the floor of the case. An unlimited number of ways to bring out the best in each individual figure may be found by studying the many ways your local jewelry, drug and department stores display small articles in their

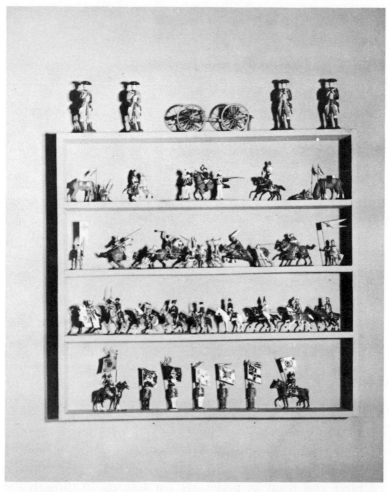

A set of wall shelves for display that can be built very easily and inexpensively. All the wood is cut to one size, and if you should not have tools get your lumber dealer to cut and square the pieces for you before delivery. This set was made from seven pieces, twenty-four inches long, three inches wide and one-half-inch thick. A box frame was constructed with four of the pieces and the other three pieces fashioned the shelves.

windows and show cases.

The props or display stands must be solid and set level so that they won't tip over with your prize figures. Beside small boxes, ordinary tin cans can be converted into very professional looking and practical display props. Used in combination with boxes or by themselves, the

Display props made from tin cans, such as these, can be used in book-cases, curio cabinets and any number of places where miniatures in the back must be raised in order not to be hidden by those in front. The cans are wrapped in colored cardboard or paper and the tops are filled with material to make them level. Novel effects can be produced by using a variety of types of cans.

round cans avoid too many sharp corners and give your display a more pleasing effect. Cans of all heights and diameters may be utilized. After being thoroughly cleaned and one end cut out with a can opener, they may be painted and used as pedestals for figures. Although the painted cans will serve the purpose in a practical manner, very little effort can turn the lowly cans into expensive looking fixtures.

After selecting a variety of sizes to suit your display space, and cutting out the bottom of each, give the cans a coat of shellac, laquer or paint. Paint the tops as well as the sides of the cans. Select colored paper, light weight cover stock (cardboard), or wall paper that has a pleasing neutral shade. Measure the distance between the beading around the top and bottom of the cans very carefully, cut strips of paper or card this width; be sure

44

to make clean straight cuts. With any good glue or cement, secure the paper around the can; either string or rubber bands may be wrapped around the cans to hold the paper until the cement dries. Many cans have embossed numbers and circles or other indentations on their tops which prevent objects from sitting level on them. This is overcome in one or two ways. First, a disc of cardboard may be cut and cemented on the top of the can. The second, and far more effective way, is to use plaster of paris. Set the cans, after wrappers have been cemented in place, on a level table. Mix plaster of paris to the consistency of heavy cream and carefully pour on the top of the can. The plaster will level itself and form a snowy white top that will make an exciting pedestal for your finest figures. Various sizes and heights can be arranged into an unlimited number of settings to accommodate as many figures as desired.

Military miniatures are not only models of soldiers,

Union Civil War artillery going into action. These tiny figures made by Robert Cardozo are in HO scale and only about one-inch tall.

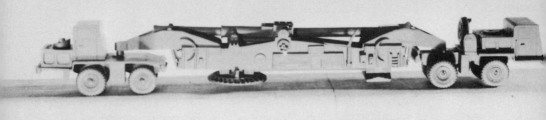

This atomic cannon is cast from metal and measures ten inches long. Many different types of tanks and cannon can be bought already made or in kits, which the hobbyist may assemble himself. This model is made by Comet Metal Products, internationally famous for its exact models of tanks, ships and aircraft.

but include models of all the tools and transportation methods used in warfare. Model airplanes, model ships and railroads as well as wagons, chariots, and models of the many other war vehicles and equipment should not be overlooked when making and collecting military miniatures. The ballista, catapult and trebuchet were just as effective and feared by the enemy in their day as the atomic cannon and guided missile today. Most certainly, Hannibal and his war elephants of the ancient world and the mangonels and espringales of the middle ages were forerunners of our modern tanks, and who can resist the thrilling history and development of warfare in the air. It takes no great stretch of imagination to compare the heraldry of the knight with the insigna, slogans and pictures painted on aircraft and tanks of modern war. Much of medieval heraldry was based on the rebus or pun, the same as the modern fighting man enjoys a little humor to lighten the seriousness of war.

Railroads, since their beginning, have played an important part in warfare not alone as carriers for troops and supplies, but as actual combatants. The great railway guns of the World Wars, the railroad battery of the American Civil War, and many others are well known. One of the most audacious exploits of the War Between the States was the daring theft of the "General" locomotive and train by James Andrews and a party of twenty-one Union enlisted men. The resulting chase and recapture of the locomotive by Confederate Captain W. A. Fuller has been woven into many tales of fact and

Ancient war machines. These models are built up piece by piece from wood just
like the real ones. The Springle which measures eight and one-half inches high and
seven and one-half inches at the base is a seige weapon that will shoot three darts
at one time. The Tower is a wall-scaling device and measures ten inches tall and
five inches at the base. Both models are fully operating.

Photo courtesy Authentic Reproductions Co.

Photo courtesy Tyler Manufacturing Company

The model of a real veteran of the Civil War, "The General", the prototype of which carried supplies and troops during the war. It is best known for the great locomotive chase involving Andrews and Fuller. Models such as this, in HO scale (3.5mm to the foot) may be bought in kits to build, or ready-built, in operating or non-operating models. Airplane, ships, tanks and locomotives are regarded as military miniatures just as much as the men who operate them.

Photo by Hinchliff

Charles A. Sweet, Jr. is shown here with some of the medals, awards and trophies he has received.

A number of military miniature clubs hold displays and competition each year inviting collectors to compete against others from all parts of the world. The hobbyists frequently do not attend the competitions in person but ship their prize figures and dioramas for display and judging; this falls in many classes such as artillery, single figures, groups and dioramas, workmanship and faithfulness in research and coloring being the important factors.

HO gage soldiers and civilians of the Civil War modeled to a scale of 3.5mm to the foot (about an eighth of an inch) which makes the figure of Lincoln a little under seven-eighths of an inch tall.

fiction. History records many events that the modeler, who likes railroads as well as soldiers, can incorporate into operating or display models. Manufacturers of model railroad equipment produce a number of kits for old and modern equipment that can be utilized in creating dioramas. By the same token, hobby stores have many varieties of airplane and ship model kits that are worthy of consideration in creating a collection of military history in miniature.

So varied are the phases of the military miniature hobby that it is truly the omnibus of creative and collecting hobbies. No matter whether your interests run to stamps, coins, model railroads, model airplanes, ships, arms, or any of the other avocations that bring relaxation to thousands of people around the globe, the miniature soldier and his weapons will add additional color and spark to your collection. The photography fan will find military miniatures willing and patient subjects, adding a whole new exciting field for his endeavors. As a hobby in itself or as a segment of another pastime, it is indeed ideal. It permits full enjoyment in large or small space and with little or much money, and the avenues of research and interest are endless.

50

CHAPTER 3

War Games

War Games are no doubt as old as wars, and wars are as ancient as man. It is reasonable to believe that in all probability the ancient veteran returning from wars re-fought the wars with his friends and young sons. While he was away at the wars, the boys and old men no doubt created imaginary battles and there is a likelihood that figures or playing pieces of some sort became involved in the game. Military leaders have always known that visual instructions are absorbed more quickly than verbal ones, and they have used representative figures through the centuries to convey tactics to their lieutenants. Frederick the Great, considered the founder of Prussian greatness, who set the pattern of military precepts for many years, was a great exponent of the war game using model soldiers in training his officers. Great military leaders, both famous and infamous, before and since the time of Frederick have respected the military miniature's value; the miniatures now play a valuable part in regular army training as well as in cadet training in leading military schools.

Chess, a game whose origin is lost in antiquity, is the best known of all war games. It has been traced back to about 200 B.C., and its origin has been attributed to many people of different races. Many games are tales of individual skill, but in few contests is the mental competition keener or more demanding than in chess, where the board is a battlefield and the playing pieces are representative of military forces. With the King and Queen and Bishops representing those who directed the wars, the agile Knights and plodding Pawns illustrating the soldiers, and the Castles or Rooks reminiscent of the huge towers constructed in ancient times as offensive platforms and defensive shields, we have the panoply of war.

Chess men have been produced from many types of materials and in an endless number of styles. Wood, ivory, precious metals, iron, clay and other substances have been carved, sculptured and cast into chess men of simple utilitarian designs, and the same variety of materials have also been used to create an endless variety of chess men ranging from the ridiculous to the sublime. Many museums and art galleries have in their collections superb and artistic sets. Collecting chess men is a hobby like collecting stamps, coins and military miniatures.

The most interesting and most representative of combative forces are chessmen carved in direct imitation of warring warriors. As we admire these carvings, we seem to be turning back the pages of history. Here in ivory are arrayed the forces of the Romans and the Goths; in another set we see the Crusaders on one side of the board and the Saracens on the other, with the kings carved in the likenesses of Richard the Lion Hearted and Saladin. Napoleon is frequently carved as a chess king; indeed the Emperor himself was an ardent player of chess, and in his final years at St. Helena would often call one of his few companions to join him at the chessboard where, as a bishop slanted over to capture a rook or a pawn edged toward a knight, the Corsican would dream back to the days of the Nile, or Moscow, or Waterloo.

A complete set of iron chessmen. In the background are Frederick the Great and Queen flanked by grenadier officers with peaked caps of the period. These grenadiers represent the bishops while the knights and rooks are the conventional horse-heads and towers. The pawns are cast in the form of peasants. Standing in the foreground are Napoleon and his Queen flanked by bishops as Old Guard officers with their tall, bearskin hats. Other pieces correspond with those on the opposite side, the pawns wearing clothing of Napoleon's time rather than that of Frederick's. It is not unusual for sets to be made representing military leaders of different periods opposing each other, as in this one, especially if the characters are famous strategists such as Frederick and Napoleon.

In the Georgetown University at Washington, there is a beautiful set carved from apple and cherry woods illustrating the forces engaged in the 30-Years War. In a Philadelphia collection, there are several military sets, one based on our Civil War, with Lincoln and Jefferson Davis as opposing leaders. Today in Russia where chess

53

is a popular game, sets are manufactured to represent the Soviet forces as opposed to those of the free world. One devotee of chess who desires that his sets convey the closest impressions of military history has engaged skilled artisans to carve for him chessmen to represent the forces engaged in the great battles of history. Marathon of ancient times, and Saratoga of our Revolution are included, and perhaps there will soon be added the invasion of Normandy or MacArthur's return to the Philippines.

Many of America's notable military leaders have been chess players. In the Smithsonian Institution, you can see the chessmen used by General George Washington, while in a case nearby are those of General George McClellan. Across the Potomac where the former home of Robert E. Lee is a national shrine, the finely-turned chess set of General Lee reposes on a tray-like chess board. During Lee's advance toward Gettysburg he was asked what he would do if some agile Northern general slipped behind him and attempted to seize Richmond. "In that case," said Lee, with his mind on Philadelphia or Washington, but thinking also of these same chessmen, "I'd trade Queens." But two years later he was checkmated at Appomatox.

Many famous writers have written about war games. Robert Louis Stevenson recorded a series of battles through which he and his stepson maneuvered lead soldiers during several winters in Switzerland. Laurence

Sterne, a British humorist of the eighteenth century, in his writings about Tristam Shandy relates a story about Uncle Toby, an invalid veteran, who with his servant Corporal Trim followed the campaigns of The Duke of Marlborough with a war game. Equipped with maps and plans of every fortified city in Flanders, Toby and Trim would eagerly await news of the Duke's latest seige operations and then construct the fortifications in minute detail with accurate terrain to exact scale. As the seige progressed they followed each approach, moving their miniature batteries and men until the fort surrendered. They even rigged up a gadget connected to a Turkish waterpipe to simulate the crossfire of the batteries.

No doubt the greatest champion of the little lead soldier and the miniature battle field was the late H. G. Wells. Wells describes "Little Wars" as a game for boys of every age from twelve to one hundred and fifty, and even older, if the limbs remain sufficiently supple, by girls of the better sort and by a few rare and gifted women. H. G. Wells was without a doubt the dean of War Games as they are played today. He was certainly responsible for bringing about more humane warfare with his book "Little Wars" in 1913, whose rules brought to an end the wholesale slaughter of lead, tin and wood soldiers with catapult, rubber band, pea shooters, marbles and other destructive tools of miniature warfare. Miniature murder, the mere setting up and knocking down of men, was stopped. The rules set down by Mr. Wells form the basis for most of the rules used today in War Games played with military miniatures. Naturally, there

This naval gun is the most popular type of artillery with war-game players. It measures seven-and-three-quarter inches long and will shoot a projectile a considerable distance with a reasonable amount of accuracy. Many other types are also used.

have been refinements, but "Little Wars" by H. G. Wells is still the primer on the subject and a basic manual for all miniature soldier tacticians and arm chair generals.

The miniature cannon, which could propel a projectile with a reasonable amount of accuracy up to several yards, came into existence in the latter part of the nineteenth century. These guns, made in a variety of sizes, are loaded from the breech and have a screw adjustment for elevation and depression so that the target can be brought into range. Guns of the same type are made today in even greater variety and naturally a number of refinements have been made on the later models. Some of today's models come with a supply of wood projectiles which are the recommended type for war games, but most are supplied with metal projectiles. The metal bullets may be used, but most players prefer to replace them with wooden ones which can be easily made from pieces of wood dowel. Since the projectile is propelled by the action of a striking plate, some players increase the realism by placing caps in the breech which sends the bullet on its way with a bang and belch of smoke from the cannon's mouth. Some commanders of miniature batteries even sand and fit wood projectiles so that they fit closely, yet will pass freely through the barrel when fired. This not only increases the accuracy of the miniature weapon, but when caps are used the explosion and expansion of gasses give more power to the projectile. As you might expect, practice and experimenting are done on miniature firing ranges by students of this theory, testing the advantages of one, two or three caps over particular ranges.

Battle fields may be laid out in a variety of ways, very simply or very elaborately. They may be set up outside on the ground, inside on the floor or on a table, and of course on sand tables or other special platforms which may be constructed for the purpose. There is no set amount of space required but, naturally, the more space available, the greater the field of play which allows for more interesting maneuvers. Buildings, hills, and trees may be made from blocks of wood, books or any available material which allows the player's active imagination to transform them into a realistic field of operation. Or actual scale model terrain, houses and trees may be used which, needless to say, add immeasurably to the fun and interest of the battle. The soldiers used are generally the regular 2⅛ inch ones, but any size figures, larger or smaller, may be used.

I have no intention to provide a fast set of rules for war games. Many innovations have been introduced since Mr. Wells first set down his rules and ideas. There are even today many players who frown on the actual shooting down of enemy troops with model artillery, and who use instead dice and circles of cardboard to indicate the radius of destruction caused by imaginary cannon fire. Instead, the following is a brief description of methods, values and moves as developed by a great number of commanders of the miniature wars, including those of today's three outstanding exponents: Ted Haskell, Herb Sherlock and Jack Scruby.

After the terrain and buildings have been prepared, placement of the opposing armies is in order. Each player may have an equal number of soldiers and artillery or one side may have more than the other when one is refighting a historic battle where there were such odds.

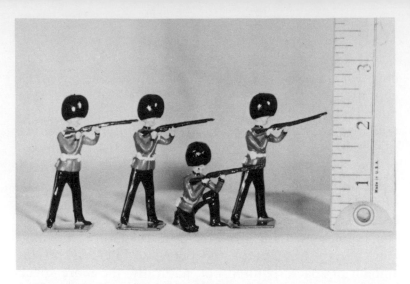

Standard two-and-one-eighth inch tall figures, the size most generally used in war games. In contests where soldiers are actually shot at with miniature weapons, inexpensive toy figures, as shown in the illustration, are used. In games where dice instead of bullets are employed, many players use fine detailed figures of the same size.

Placement of the troops to open the battle is next in order. If available, a curtain or screen is drawn midway on the field and each commander then places his men and equipment along the back line of the playing field; when the opposing commanders have their troops in place, the curtain is removed and the battle begins. However, if it is inconvenient to use a screen while placing troops in position, a roll of dice or flip of a coin may be used to decide which player will first put his men in position, after which the second player places his men in position and the battle is started. Some players take their battles more seriously and prepare maps of the terrain in advance; a copy is given to each player at least a week in advance. Each commander can then lay his battle plans before the actual time arrives. On the day or night of battle, the players set up their troops behind a drawn curtain in the same manner as mentioned previously. True, just as in real life, well-laid plans many times go astray and end in defeat, but by the same token some tacticians of the miniature battle field claim many a victory has been gained through well-laid plans. Battles of pre-planned type usually last four or five hours, and

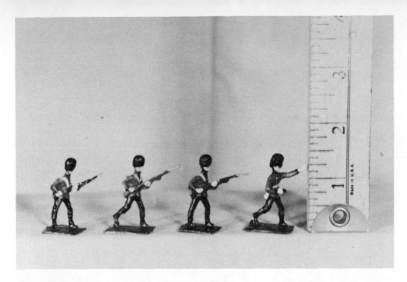

When space is at a premium many war-game players solve the problem by using small, very inexpensive full round figures as shown here. Flats are also used to carry on war games in a small-table area.

as only part of a campaign they have a particular objective, such as the taking of a road junction or river crossing; this overlaps with the next battle to be fought in the campaign.

Movement of troops and equipment as well as the fire power must be decided. For example, infantrymen can be moved not more than a certain distance during a player's turn and there is another limit of distance for cavalrymen (naturally further than the infantrymen, because they are mounted). Movement limitations and number of shots must also be decided for artillery pieces as well as the number of artillerymen required with the piece at time of moving and firing. The same applies to trains, crack troops, medics and the signal corps, along with the particular officers and men that have special power. Time limits for each move must also be set so that the game moves along and rules must be followed to decide when a soldier is killed and also who can capture whom and how captured men can be liberated and brought back into the battle.

As I mentioned earlier, H. G. Wells set down the basic rules around which most modern war games are designed. The following is a brief outline of Mr. Wells'

59

A Napoleonic battle about to start in the home of John Scruby. Mr. Scruby has designed a number of games with lead soldiers of various sizes, and has also originated a number of innovations in rules that have been adopted by war-game players all over the world.

Who says the infantry can't stop the cavalry? We shall know after the next roll of the dice. This is an exciting moment in one of John Scruby's war games.

ideas on fighting a miniature battle. One minute was allowed to move thirty men and a minute to move a gun; for example, four minutes to move sixty men and two guns. The player stood at least a yard behind his rear line and moved into action, moving his troops and weapons at the word "Go" from the timekeeper and then withdrew from action immediately on the word "Time" from the timekeeper when the allotted time was up. The competing player then proceeded in the same manner. No artillery fire was allowed until after the first player had made two moves. In order to fire or move an artillery piece, it had to have at least four men on its own side within six inches of the weapon and if the player fired the piece it had to be done before moving any troops. The gun could be fired or moved during the player's turn, but not both. If fired, the player was allowed four shots and any of his own troops in line of fire were permitted to lie down to avoid being killed by fire from his own side. Although the gun couldn't be moved, it could be turned on its axis to line up the target. After firing, the gun was left in position and two men had to be placed at the end of the trail directly behind the wheels. Should the player elect to move his guns instead of firing, he was allowed to move the weapon the same distance as the men serving it were permitted to move at one time. Infantry men were allowed to be moved up to one foot at a time and cavalrymen were allowed to move up to two feet. Four men were required to move with the gun and be placed within six inches of it.

Each player was provided with a measuring string to facilitate troop movements (one foot for infantry, two feet for cavalry) and players were required to keep their men clear of trees and buildings. A distance of at least one-sixteenth of an inch was also required between men. Naturally all men knocked over by artillery shots were dead, and the first man hit by an artillery shell, even if it didn't knock him over, was also dead. If the shell glanced off something and hit him, or just rolled to his feet, he was dead. No, the game was not all artillery fire. There was hand to hand fighting in which men were killed and prisoners taken as well as artillery pieces captured. If less than half of a player's army got more than the distance of a move away from the main body it was considered isolated; this could be one or more men. If the opposing player could move any of his men into contact with figures of the isolated group, a melee resulted and all soldiers within a radius of six inches of the contacted men had to take part in the fight. If it turned up that each side had an equal number of combatants in the melee, both groups were wiped out because each soldier killed a soldier and was killed himself in turn. However, if one force had more soldiers in the fight than the enemy, prisoners were taken in this fashion. The force taking prisoners had to be exactly double the number of prisoners taken — each force killed each other, man for man, until one force was double the other. For example, if eleven men attack nine, seven men would be killed and the remaining four of the superior force would take the two remaining of the inferior force prisoner. Eight against five would result in six captors and three prisoners, six against five would result in two captors and one prisoner.

Captured prisoners were then disarmed and moved under escort to the rear, or to any place the captor desired. One man could escort up to seven prisoners and had to remain within six inches of his prisoners. The prisoners could be liberated by killing the escort; however, the released prisoners could not join the fight until they had returned to their own rear lines, the "Repo-Depot" as the modern G.I. says, to be rearmed. All of this gives only an inkling of the fascinating action that was involved in Mr. Wells' little games of war. There were fights to the finish where the leaden soldiers marched into the open and slugged it out, and there were the strategic infiltration and circumventive type of tactics employed to capture the enemy's rear line to win victory. The book "Little Wars" may be seen at most public libraries and can be bought from many book dealers and dealers in military miniatures. It is an intriguing book that will fire the imagination of any man who is young in heart.

Real soldiers can't last very long without food and ammunition, and horses must have forage; so table top field marshalls must see that their troops are supplied too. Both Robert Louis Stevenson and H. G. Wells were aware of this supply problem and they, as well as today's miniature war generals, devised various ways of getting food and ammunition to the front. The following is one system used in today's war games. Supply depots are established at the start of the battle and model wagons are loaded with supplies; these wagons then follow the troops. Supplies are represented by small sticks or any other small items that can be loaded into the wagons, and each item is considered one unit. Units should be of such size that twenty can be loaded to a wagon. The supplies are then used by the troops in this manner: when a volley is fired each four men use up one unit; this also holds true when they engage in a melee — each four men use up one unit. When a field gun is fired three units are used. Another method or set of rules stretches supplies out longer by using only one unit of supply for thirty men every six moves, one unit for each six horses, and one unit of ammunition for each thirty men that fire with six consecutive moves. Naturally, if the enemy gets between the men and the supply wagons, the troops can't get supplies. The supply wagons can also be captured by killing their escorts, and supply wagons may be disabled in artillery barrages. The rules in supply as in firing are greatly varied and are decided by the different groups of enthusiasts.

The realistic action that can be brought into the game is unlimited. Entrenchments can be made as well as gun emplacements, and even mines can be laid to blow up troops and supply trains, all covered by special rules.

The actual shooting of the troops with the little cannon is still practiced by many groups of war game generals;

Photograph by Hinchliff

Looking from the British, Hessian and Tory side in Charles Sweet's American Revolution war game. The Northumberland Fusileers and Black Watch are in the foreground; Hessian Yagers are charging around the court house, and the Royal Artillery is in action by the side of the road; grenadiers and Von Rall of Hesse Cassel march up the road, Hesse Hanau artillery is emplaced on the rise to the left of the grenadiers (out of the picture); the Seventeenth Light Dragoons are charging up the road while the Tenth Foot and Tarleton's Dragoons are in reserve in the foreground.

The scenic backdrop intensifies the interest of the game; the trees are set in clay so they can be moved at will in setting up a variety of battlefields.

however, there are a large number of players who frown on the actual use of the gun. This situation exists no doubt for a number of reasons. Recent years have seen the growth of interest in the model military figure that is correct in scale and uniform. The collectors and makers of these finer figures, who are also war game enthusiasts, naturally aren't interested in shooting projectiles at

65

War game set up by Charles A. Sweet, Jr. representing a battle of the American Revolution. In this picture you are looking from the American and French side. Thompson's Pennsylvania Rifles are coming over the stone bridge and Morgan's Rifles are standing on the wooden bridge; Lamb's Artillery and a Continental Navy gun crew are in action on the ridge; the 3rd New Jersey and Wayne's Light Infantry are charging around the court house; Baylor's Dragoons are charging down the road; Haslett's Delaware, Lauzun's French Legion and Gatinois French Grenadiers are in reserve behind the stone bridge. Roads, bridges, buildings are laid out on the squared-off playing table.

models in which they have invested an amount of time and money. These same people also have in their collections non-operating scale model cannon that are more detailed than the spring-operating ones, which in most cases sacrifice scale and detail for operation; so there is no artillery on the field that will actually shoot. Another reason for the non-shooting war game is lack of space. In the shooting war game a fair amount of space is needed because of the firing range of the guns; in the non-shooting game, however, not only the firing range, but also the movement of troops can be scaled down. In fact, very satisfactory games can be played on an ordinary kitchen table and even on a card table. One old-timer says he prefers the non-shooting war because his knees don't bend as well as they used to, and it's much easier to roll dice than bend down to aim a cannon.

As you might suspect, in the non-shooting game measurements become very important, since the effect of fire power must be calculated instead of shooting projectiles. The amount of space available for the battlefield will naturally govern the measurements. Should the battle field be laid out, for example, in a space six feet by four feet, you would decide first the length of movement for troops. A practical infantry move on this size field would be six inches, and for cavalry twelve inches. Naturally these moves are reduced if less space is used; for example, the infantry move would be two inches on a battlefield the size of a normal card table. Cannon range on the 6 x 4 field should be set at something between two and three feet, and a stick cut to measure the decided range. Any troops beyond the decided distance would be out of range and could not be killed by the cannon fire. To use artillery on the enemy, the player must point out the troops that are being fired on, check the range with the measuring stick, and then roll one dice; the number that comes up will be the number of men killed by the shot. A cannon may be fired only once during a player's move. In most games only soldiers fully or partially exposed can be killed, because the cannon fire is considered direct line firing and not high trajectory as with a howitzer or mortar. However, rules can be worked out for howitzer and mortar fire if the players wish.

The rules for the hand to hand fighting in the non-shooting game are the same as previously described for the game where spring-fired artillery is used. Small arms may be used in both volley fire and skirmisher fire in the following manner. A volley may be fired if a player can line up a minimum of six of his soldiers shoulder to shoulder (bases touching) and within a range of one

Mr. Wells has developed his game so that the country over which the campaign is to be fought is out rivers, streams and fords, cardboard forts, barracks, houses, and what not; there are employed leade nine times out of ten at a distance of nine yards, and having a screw adjustment for elevation and depr a curtain across it for a short time, so that the general of each opposing army may dispose of his force All moves of man and guns are timed. An infantryman moves not more than a foot at a time, a cavalr Mr. Wells is seen on the left of the drawing, taking a measurement with a length of string, to determine t beginning the game.

ny desired manner, with the aid of branches of shrubs as trees, with cardboard bridges, rocks, chalked-
n and cavalrymen, and guns firing wooden cylinders about an inch long, capable of hitting a toy soldier
e are strict rules governing the combat. Before a battle begins, the country is divided by the drawing of
e enemy's being aware of that disposition. Then the curtains are drawn back and the campaign begins.
re than two feet, and a gun, according to whether cavalry or infantry are with it, from one to two feet.
some of his forces may move. On the right and left are seen the curtains for dividing the country before

move or less from the troops to be fired upon. The player must point out to his opponent the soldiers being fired upon and then roll one dice. The number on the dice is the number of enemy killed by the volley, which may be from one to six. Just as in cannon fire, troops fired upon must be fully exposed, or at least, have head and shoulders exposed, in order to be killed. If the player can line up more than six soldiers shoulder to shoulder, he may fire a volley for each six in line, but must indicate soldiers being fired upon with each volley. Should both sides come into position to fire a volley at the same time, the volleys will kill one out of every four men on each side, and then one side must fall back one move. Each player, after removing the dead, rolls one dice, then multiplies the number on the dice by the number of soldiers still alive in his volley line. The player having the higher total holds his position while the player with the lower total falls back. While only soldiers on the front rank of a group may fire, all soldiers in the unit are counted in deciding the total and must fall back or hold the position as indicated.

In skirmisher fire any number of men can engage any number of the enemy within a range of one move. There are no casualties in skirmisher fire; the results are only in one group losing ground. The decision on which side moves back is made in the same manner as in deciding which side moves back in the volley exchange, with each side rolling a dice and multiplying it by the number of men in the action. However, where the skirmishers exchange fire with a volley line, the skirmishers suffer one casualty for each four men in the volley line, but the volley line suffers no casualties from the skirmishers' fire. The players again decide who loses ground, either the skirmishers or the volley line, by the same dice method. The usual procedure is to decide the situation after each man's alternate move. A player's move is begun by firing artillery, then moves are made, and the results of hand-to-hand fighting, skirmishes and volleys are worked out.

Herbert A. Sherlock deep in the planning of a strategic war game move. Mr. Sherlock's battles are all built around the Civil War, and battlefields are laid out on a series of squared boards which may be set up on a group of card tables or on any flat surface.

Closeup of a sector in the war games designed by Herbert Sherlock. The boards are ruled off in one-inch squares and the roads, streams and other physical features are drawn on the boards with chalk to indicate the particular terrain of the battle. White puffs in the picture are shell bursts made of cotton; dead and wounded lie on the field. Interest is added to the game by using figures in natural action poses. Marching figures are exchanged for those in fighting positions when troops move into action; dead and wounded figures replace those shot in action.

A number of players may participate in this game, each contestant being the commander of a certain number of figures and responsible for their movement, taking orders from the commander-in-chief who may be in another room sending his orders by written dispatch to his field commanders.

War games may be played by two or more players and may become quite elaborate — for example, one designed and played by an American Civil War enthusiast and his friends. The playing field is laid out on a table eighty-four inches by fifty-six inches and is ruled off in one inch squares. When a battle is to be fought, houses and roads, rivers and creeks, fences and hills are laid out as close to the original Civil War battlefield as possible. The armies are composed of cavalry, infantry, artillery and a supply train. The infantry consists of ten brigades and each fighting man and officer is duplicated by a marching man. They are marched onto the field to make contact with the enemy and then men in fighting positions are substituted for the marching men.

The cavalry consists of two divisions with a commander-in-chief. The artillery is made up of five batteries of one gun each, four being smooth-bore Napoleons and one being a rifled Parrot with a longer range. The Union side uses four Corps Commanders and the South two or three, depending on which battle is being fought. The brigades make up the divisions which form the Corps.

The Commanding General operates from a small map about twenty-one inches by fourteen inches in another room. He moves pieces of colored board on his map according to his plans and sends written orders to his Corps Commanders and receives their written reports. Each type of man has his maximum move of so many squares, and opponents are killed by rifle, pistol, bayonet, saber and artillery fire. Models of dead men and horses replace the models of living figures as casualties occur, this adds immensely to the game. Moves by each side are made by a clock laid out in ten minute intervals, and all orders and reports are marked as to time.

Each side can have a Commander-in-Chief, Corps Commanders, Cavalry Commanders and Artillery Commanders if enough players turn out. The game resembles chess and a player must be observant and use his skill because there is no luck involved. A percentage of loss to the whole or loss of a supply train governs the battle.

Each side numbers about one hundred and thirty figures, and battles may be fought either with the sides even or in proportion to the sizes of the contending armies in the Civil War.

There is here, as in the description of the shooting war game, no intention of trying to give you a set of fast rules and all the exciting phases of fighting miniature wars. For one reason, there are no set rules and much depends on the decisions of local groups of enthusiasts; for another reason, it would take an entire book to give a description of the many moves and rules that have been developed by the various groups. However, the principles of the game are sufficiently explained in the foregoing so that you can try your hand at fighting a miniature battle. There is no doubt that you will find this one of the most fascinating segments of making and collecting military miniatures. After learning the basic principles, you and your friends will no doubt add exciting innovations and rules that will afford you many hours of fun and relaxation.

CHAPTER 4

Table Top Photography

Inevitably there comes a time in the life of every military miniature collector when he looks at the snapshots of his favorite miniatures with a feeling that someone or something has not done right by his pride and joy. His magnificent model of General Custer looks like a dime store plastic. Thus, he starts looking for an inexpensive means of improving his photographic efforts.

At this point he encounters the genuine table top photographer, who is not a collector, but who uses military miniatures as the principal actors in the dramas he stages on the family tea table, or any large flat surface he can find unoccupied by his wife, his children or the family cat. If the military miniature collector has already gone into the field of dioramas, some phases of table top photography will be familiar. There is, however, one very fundamental difference: the diorama is made to be viewed by the human eye, which makes charitable allowances for imperfections. The table top setting is made to be viewed by the unrelenting eye of the camera lens which, not only makes no allowance for imperfections, but generally seems

Colonel Franklin E. and Franklin T. Jordan, a father-and-son team of table-top photographers, are camera hobbyists who have found military miniatures to be exciting subjects. They have blended, with unusual success, photographs of miniatures with motion pictures taken on actual battlefields. Ideas and suggestions in the chapter "Table-top Photography" were contributed by this team.

to take a fiendish delight in portraying them vividly.

You can usually tell a table top photographer by his look of quiet desperation. Fate seems to endow his miniature figures with all the perverse traits of humans. It takes hours to compose a table top that initially appeared to require only minutes. The genuine table top photographer has learned by exacting, exasperating experience that patience is not only a virtue, but an essential ingredient of his hobby.

There are, in general, three types of table top photographers: realists, unrealists or dealers in fantasy, and those in between who, for the lack of a more definitive description, might be called representationalists. The representationalist produces the fascinating designs and portrayals that make illustrations for such things as magazine articles, book jackets, book plates, letter heads, bill heads and the like.

The realist is frequently a student of history. His table top photography results from hours of research in dusty archives in search of a significant or hidden truth which will fire him with enthusiasm to portray it. He hopes the viewer will feel his emotional fire and share its warmth. The task of the realist isn't easy. It is a rare historic photograph that will serve as a model, and if the photograph is that good, why bother with a miniature of it? Usually, many photos are needed and, collectively, the story is only partially told. History, before the advent of photography, depended upon artists' drawings. Any historian who has ever checked such drawings against the recorded descriptions realizes that the "On-The-Scene" artists have already taken all the liberties the record will stand. To copy them would be fatal. The realist has no pictorial source material and must translate from the written word. Since for most battles there are innumerable conflicting accounts, this is no arm chair task.

For those gifted with imagination, fantasy offers more fun. All the illusions the realist must create are not required. On the other hand, to tell an essential and important truth through fantasy is more of a mental job than most persons care to tackle. The result is that much table top photography is a curious mixture of fantasy and realism. But whatever the approach, the table top photograph which does not convey to the viewer some mood or emotion is hardly worth the effort.

When skillfully done, table top photography can turn military miniatures into entrancing giants and, by experienced blending of lights and focus, diminish or eliminate some imperfections that are evident even to the untrained eye. When that happens, the military miniature collector, who hitherto has been feeling like a combat photographer for a lost cause, knows the exultation of victory and the feeling that table top photography is worth the effort.

It is not an accident that the common expression in photography is to "Shoot" a picture. The camera is your artillery piece and your table top composition your target. A gun without a target usually winds up as a decoration on the village green. A camera without a target is equally as useless. So before I discuss the equipment needed for table top photography, consideration will be given to the target, which in this case will be military miniatures.

There are three essential elements of the target: the miniatures, the table top and the back drop. The latter separates your creation from the illusion-destroying reality of the conventional household objects which surround your table top.

Now we come to the secret of the successful table top photographers' art. By choice, he does not use a table top at all. All he wants of the table is to have the legs and the frame. On this he erects his stage, which may be one level, but usually, if representing the terrain of a military maneuver, it will rise and fall with the contours of the ground. Most interiors have some type of split levels. What the table top photographer wants is a generous supply of assorted sizes of light lumber and wire mesh. By choice, also, the table top photographer wants a table frame as wide as he can conveniently reach across and as long as his room permits. This is seldom enough room for his projects. Battle scenes are usually difficult to portray. In the Civil War, for example, an active fighting front might be as long as two or three miles. with the troop concentrations representing nearly as much again in depth. To portray even a significant fraction of this area in a rectangle about a yard wide and two yards long becomes an engineering feat of space defying illusion.

This is not the only problem. If you place enough men in the setting to even approximate the actual numbers, they will have to be extremely small. Then your final photographic print will have to be the size of a post office mural to have any emotional impact at all. The illusion must be created by the absolute minimum of figures in the smallest possible area; and you have set yourself a first class problem in table top logistics when you tackle this.

There are three divisions to your table top: the foreground, middle distance (or transition area) and the background. The standard military miniature size (2⅛ inches tall) provides sturdy actors for your foregrounds, but in many instances you will want half-size figures for the middle area. You will find that "full formed" figures are not required in this area and that "flats," which are about an inch and a quarter tall, will work out very well. Smaller figures still may be required for the background in some compositions.

Normally, however, background figures and scenery may be paintings or photographs, depending upon the type of background used. An artist's painting or a photographic enlargement can be the backdrop and portray the exact scene desired. Even more effective is the use of a large ground glass, which can be ordered through any photographic store. Using this as a background, you can, by rear projection of a color slide, create the specific terrain desired. This is more complicated than other methods since it requires a separate exposure for foreground and background, but it is the technique used by

TV and the movies to make what "ain't" look real. For all its complications, it is cheaper than hiring a professional scenery painter every time you want a new set. For semi-realism and fantasy, a neutral background of a plain substance such as paper, wood, masonite or similar material will do. By variations in the textures, the patterns or the lighting, these backgrounds can be made to harmonize with the foreground effect. A particularly pleasing effect can be obtained by what is called differential focusing or throwing out of focus all except the central figures.

At this point you must recognize the limitations of your miniatures. While the size is reduced, the relative weight and other physical characteristics of the materials do not change. The easiest way to convince yourself is to try to make a miniature waterfall look like a real one by using real water. There are those who claim it can be done, but if you have any other use for a considerable amount of time and money, you will end up with a more willing substitute and leave water to the kitchen sink.

Fortunately, problems of scale and perspective can be overcome to a large extent by the selection of your camera viewpoint and your lighting emphasis. These technical controls will be discussed later.

Composition determines the ultimate value of your target. A sound course in artistic appreciation is the best preparation but, in lieu thereof, it can be learned by your own observation and analysis at the local museum of art, with perhaps an assist by an elementary book on the subject from the local public library. Grouping is extremely important. What looks like a mass of soldiers on the table top may turn out on the negative to have sizable areas of uninspiring emptiness. On the other hand, too tight a massing will blend essential action into an indistinguishable tangle of arms and legs.

Fortunately for table top photography, closeup pictures make foreground objects appear relatively larger. The danger, however, is that they may be not only larger, but distorted. It is equally important that when

80

a figure is shown, the entire figure is in focus and that an arm or leg too near the camera is not blurred. While it is essential that your composition be correct at lens level, and not at your eye level, you must remember that with reflex cameras the image is reversed, and you must always keep in mind whether your figure is right-handed or left-handed. Observe too, which limb, if raised, obscures the least if a choice is available.

Action is a powerful factor in creating an emotion, but some of the powerful flow of movement is lost when action is frozen, reduced, and copied in miniature. When this reproduction is again copied and changed from three dimensions to one, you are thankful if any illusion of the original remains.

For test shots, a polaroid camera is a great advantage. In spite of much experience, patient arrangements and checking, and critical observation, only a trial photograph will reveal hidden flaws. A polaroid camera will do it quickly and is entirely adequate for discovering deficiencies. To see a print of your creation a minute after you have finished it is a thrill in itself.

Equipment for table top photography can be comparatively simple and inexpensive, or complex and correspondingly expensive. The camera is the artillery piece and the film its ammunition. Light and lens determine speed or velocity. A camera which will provide ground glass focusing is essential. The single or twin reflex may be used for some shots, but for real closeups the ground glass is a must. Many cameras are made so the film roll back can be removed and an adapter back for ground glass inserted, as well as an adapter for cut film. Viewing through the top lens of a reflex camera will not show the effect achieved by manipulation of the diaphram on the lower lens. The effects from these different depths of focus may make or break a picture.

A modern sturdy tripod is also essential and it should have a central column so that the legs do not have to be moved to adjust height. On top of the column should be a 90-degree tilting head, and the tripod should be sufficiently weighted to eliminate any danger of accidental upset. Frequently, when the desired angle for your "battle" has been obtained by adjusting the tripod, the upright lines in the picture on the ground glass will appear to be converging. In some cases this illusion of perspective will be an advantage, but in most cases it is better eliminated.

The table top photographer who wishes to make the investment will have an advantage in using a Studio View camera with a long extension bellows, rise-fall adjustments, swing tilt and a reversible back. With this equipment, distortions can be corrected, and desired composition attained. The 4x5 size is very practical for table top photography, and the cost of even a new Studio View camera in this size will not be too much strain on the serious hobbyist's budget. These cameras use individual cut film in film holders. One shot can be taken and processed for study, corrections made, and then the final shots taken. Since one scene may represent scores of hours of research, procurement of target items, composition and technical arrangements, this single shot approach is highly recommended. This is especially true if color is being shot. Although it represents more work, better results can be obtained by shooting your color on a 4x5 film and then reducing it to 35mm. or 2x2. In the copying you can crop and eliminate some undesirable sections, and you can also vary your color emphasis to get the most pleasing results. Enlargements from 4x5 black and white present no special problems.

Choice of film brand is a personal matter. There are many good ones on the market. Since you have no movement to contend with, emulsion speed is not a factor and slower films can be used. Unless you intend your photographs solely for publication, you do not need a very high contrast film. The important thing is to match your developer to your film for the most pleasing results. Once you find the combination, stick to it.

Books could be, and have been, written solely on lighting for photography. Military miniature collectors planning to add table top photography to their skills should study a good book on the subject, along with other photographic texts which may be found at any photographic supply store. Since the subjects will wait patiently for your exposure, there is no need for flash equipment and all the lighting needs can be met with flood and spot lights. The minimum lights needed are two flood lights and one baby spot light. If you are going to work in color you will want more equipment, particularly a voltage meter and voltage regulator to keep your lights constant, since a growing America is outdistancing its power lines, and 115 volts home current will vary sometimes as low as 105 or as high as 125 volts. To conserve the life of your flood lights, a control box that cuts them to half voltage while making changes or set adjustments is well worth its cost. It is important too, not to "cook" your set, as some of your miniature props may not stand up under prolonged heat. Number 1 type flood lights are large enough.

One flood light can do many things if you supplement it with various reflecting surfaces such as mirrors, plyboard covered with crinkled aluminum foil, or white blotting paper. The lights themselves can be diffused even by a handkerchief, placed safely in front of the light, or the light may be "bounced" from walls or ceiling. Remember the word photograph means literally "light writing," or as the more poetic call it "painting with light". Each milliphot light unit of illumination on your target is like a drop of paint. Whether you photograph in color or not, your military miniatures and sets should be finished in natural color. Modern panchromatic film reveals true colors by intermediate tones of gray even in monochrome prints, and false colors are very noticeable. There are two methods of emphasizing or de-emphasizing colors. One is to put filters on the lights and the other a filter on the camera lens. Since you use only one lens and usually several lights for blending purposes, light filters will serve you well, but lens filters are often essential. A polaroid screen for your lens is highly useful since many objects of war are polished metals that frequently cast distracting reflections. A good booklet on the use of filters is recommended for study.

In simulated night battle photography, greater realism is achieved if the lights are more in proportion to the size of the figures. A model railroad transformer, which will furnish 6, 12, 18 and 24 volts and has a rheostat control so the lights can be dimmed, is very valuable. Lights as small as a grain of wheat can be purchased at most Model Shops and when placed in the setting provide some highly damatic effects. Cellophane can be used to cover these little bulbs, since they do not run hot, and as all types of colors obtained.

Once you have a composition and lighting effect that looks appealing on the ground glass, you want the equipment to translate the photrons into foot candles of light. This is done by an exposure meter from which the various shutter speeds and diaphram combinations can be determined. In table top work, where you make the diaphram part of your distance control, let the speed be what it may since it makes little difference to you whether the exposure is one-fifth of a second, five seconds or five minutes. A quality exposure meter is essential and you will never regret the investment. Be sure it will measure both reflected and incident light. The objects you are photographing sometimes are hard to measure, because the reflection varies appreciably. Hence for critical color work, you should obtain a neutral test card from your photo supply store. One side of the card is gray and reflects 18% of the light shed on it. You can read the light reflected from it directly from your meter. In dim illumination you can use the white side of the card which reflects 90%. Then divide your meter reading by five. In general, the ratio of meter readings between your major floodlights and your spot light or side flood light should not be more than 4 to 1, and preferably 3 to 1. In addition to this check, readings should be taken of the darkest section where you want some detail to show and the brightest spot where you want some detail that is not "burned" out. This ratio should be in the neighborhood of 3 or 4 to 1. The overall picture can be light or dark, but the ratio within it must stay within bounds.

In World War II, artillery experts worked out a target shattering system called "TOT" or time-on-target whereby, after innumerable calculations at a given instant, someone pushed the signal and from scores of cannon, projectiles sped toward the target to arrive and detonate simultaneously. By the time you have made and checked all the technical adjustments, you sometimes wish that when you pressed the camera cable there would be one soul satisfying explosion. Instead you push the button and then cut the lights. You stand there stunned in the silence of the gloom wondering what, if anything, you have on the film to compensate for your hours of work and anticipation.

In artillery, in spite of all calculations the one sure means of a hit is to bracket your target. You shoot over, then under, then left, then right and finally you are on it. It is well worth your time and effort to calculate your exposure and then bracket your target. One shot on calculation, another one stop above, and another one stop below it, and one of the three latent images on your films should have the makings of what you saw when you dreamed up the idea many moons before.

There is a decided letdown if at this point you have to wrap up your film holders and take them to your nearest photo finisher. Neither the equipment nor the skill required to develop your own film is complicated. A developing outfit including a contact printer is very inexpensive and you can see the results of your handiwork in a half-hour after you have taken the picture. The home kits for developing color films require only patience and the ability to follow faithfully simple directions. Nothing quite matches the thrill of seeing your battle in full color emerge on film. A word of warning to the novice when he does his first color film; after development and you hang the film up to dry, it looks as if it is spoiled. It is a dull dirty reddish color on one side, and a pallid dull blue on the other. Don't throw it away; let it dry until morning and you will think it is beautiful.

Maybe you are starting to think the equipment represents more than you want to spend on table top photography. While photography is, in itself, a hobby and the proper tools have much to do with the final product, there are many improvisations that can be made. A simple camera, floor lamps and a card table make a start. The idea and its staging still make the picture.

For focusing a roll film camera, the back can be taken off and a piece of ground glass (obtained inexpensively from any large photographic supply house) can be cut to fit in the film plane. Even tissue paper may be used, if ground glass is not available. With today's fast films and the most inexpensive camera, the lens can be stopped down enough to give a picture that is sharp from its foreground to its backdrop. Supplementary lens adaptors, which are inexpensive, enable the fitting of close up lenses to most inexpensive cameras. By making accurate distance measurements and using the tables that come with such lenses, even ground glass focusing can be eliminated, although this is not recommended.

There are many books at your photographic supply store suggesting hundreds of adaptations which convert simple cameras for more complex operations, they show how to construct and improvise tripods, lens shades, lights and controls, and darkrooms. For example, the ball and socket for a camera can be purchased separately and inexpensively and fitted to any weighted object such as an old flat iron. Then you will have a table top tripod for next to nothing.

A diffusion screen for a light in a metal reflector can be made by using two spring type paper clips and two wire coat hangers which are bolted to the springs. A piece of tracing cloth is cut so that no light will pass around it when it is about six inches in front of the reflector. The clip handles will angle the wire frame outward and hold the cloth tight, yet far enough away to eliminate fire danger.

Lens shades can be made from almost any pliable substance such as paper, press-board, leather or metal. A common kitchen funnel can have its snout cut off and fitted to a lens adaptor for use as a sun shade. Sunshades, incidentally, are very useful to keep stray light out of the lens in table top work.

Where there's a will there's a way. The first thing to do when your interest is aroused in table top photography is to visit your nearest photographic store and buy several of the good books and pamphlets on photographic copying which is the basis of table top photography. While there, inquire when and where the nearest camera club has a meeting. Attend the meeting; photographers are fellow hobbyists and you will be welcome even without an introduction. And you may be sure that among the members you will find someone who can tell you exactly how to adapt whatever photographic equipment you have, or what you have to buy to get started, no matter if your pocketbook is fat or lean at the moment.

When your photographic problems are solved, you will still be studying your target problems. Each battle scene will provide a new problem in the texture of your figures and props. You will become acutely conscious of the grain of materials, whether metals, wood or plastics, and how each one photographs. You will study colors with an intensity you never believed possible, and discover nothing is truly black or white. You will see color in the shadow and highlight. You will learn to see the almost imperceptible change in a shadow made by the addition of a faint wisp of reflected light. You will learn how a few properly placed soldiers can suggest an entire company, and you will learn the various positions for these models best to simulate action. You will learn the angle and the amount of light needed to emphasize or de-emphasize a particular feature of a model, and how the individual model is best blended with the mass. Most of this will be by trial and error, since every new setting you create will have its own special problems.

The field of military miniatures is so vast that you will do well to specialize as quickly as possible. By taking one era and the soldiers and costumes of that era, you become familiar more quickly with the problems of form and color peculiar to the models. Models from one scene fit into parts of another and this naturally helps to conserve your hobby budget. Should you select the American Civil War, for example, you will soon discover you are not alone; there are several thousands or maybe tens of thousands of other hobbyists interested in the same period, and you realize that the Civil War is far from over. This has a decided advantage because more models and more props are available on the market, and you can buy rather than build most of the miniatures you need.

There are many eras for you to explore: the ancient world, medieval period, Napoleonic wars, and many others. Even the United States, which is a peaceful nation, has averaged a war or engagement of some type every ten years during its military history. All in all, the field is full of opportunities for the table top photographer. If you are just starting on photography, remember it is a very complex hobby, if you intend to graduate from the snapshot stage. You will have to study not one, but many text books, or learn the hard way. But once you have combined collecting military miniatures with photography you will have enough of a hobby to last several lifetimes.

CHAPTER **5**

Dioramas and Scenery

Visions of great leaders and battles start to form in the collector's mind even before he has finished painting his first miniature soldier. He is suddenly on the fields of Waterloo giving advice to Napoleon, with Pickett at Gettysburg, or with Custer at Little Big Horn. Vivid panoramic flashes of shells and rockets, heroism and cowardice, gorgeous uniforms and tattered rags, the jubilation of the victor and the sorrow of the vanquished — all this and more comes alive in the collector's mind as the figure he is creating becomes more life-like with each stroke of his brush. It is only natural that the collector has a desire to use his military miniatures to depict a particular incident, so that even those who do not collect military miniatures will be able to see history in three dimension and share his enthusiasm. For, although a hobby is a personal thing, its joys and pleasures are increased a hundredfold when it can be shared with others.

A diorama is often thought of as a great stage covering a vast amount of space that the average home or modern apartment could not accommodate. This, however, is not true. A diorama is a scene that tells a story, and this may be done within a few square inches with even one or

In this reproduction of the 9th U. S. Infantry marching into Peiping in the Boxer Rebellion of 1900, built by John Scheid, the Allied forces are drawn up in review (no basis in fact) as a means of showing various uniforms. The uniform designs were copied from photographs in the National Archives taken by a United States Volunteer captain on the spot, and the uniform colors were supplied by Colonel Frederick P. Todd. United States Marines stand on the wall of the city alongside the impaled heads of Boxer leaders. The wall of the city was made smaller than scale in order to fit the diorama into a particular display space.

two figures and scenery, or it can involve hundreds of square feet and thousands of figures that could not be housed in anything smaller than the exhibition hall at your local county fair. In fact, the smaller dioramas often get their point across better than the large complicated ones, and they most certainly are more welcome in the home.

In making a small diorama you should select a particular event from history and portray the action, while using the minimum number of figures possible, with the feature character or characters overshadowing all other

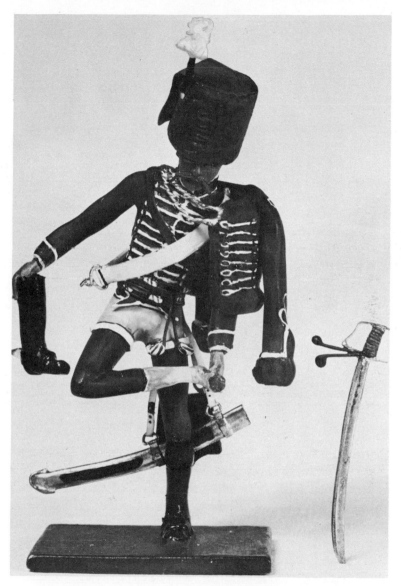

Even the cavalry gets holes in its socks. Although this unusual model, made by Frank Conley, is just one figure, you can stretch the point and call it diorama because it is a picture-telling story. The purist can put a few bushes around if he wants to make it official. Worthy of note are the small rings and straps, and the way the saber separates itself from the scabbard.

This interesting Biblical diorama, made by Robert Cardozo, shows Sampson in chains on the mountain. Mr. Cardozo works in HO scale (3.5mm to the foot) and casts all his own original figures, which are only about one-inch tall; however the detail is extremely good. In his collection are a number of bible scenes, which can be excellent for depicting.

figures and props. The action displayed on the small diorama should show just one event or action and, if it is portrayed with skill, the active mind of the viewer will complete the picture. History is full of outstanding events as well as equally important events that, although not as well known, will still furnish the bases for small dioramas. "Sergeant Ewart of the Scots Greys capturing the eagle at Waterloo," "Washington at Valley Forge," "General John Gordon, CSA, giving water to the wounded General Francis Barlow, USA, on the fields of Gettysburg," "Burnside riding the railroad handcar" — these are only a few of the many exciting events you will find throughout military history that lend themselves to the making of small dioramas. There may even be events in your own

This group of dioramas was made by Leon Chodnicki, each one mounted on a small board measuring about two and a half by six inches. He created these effective little scenes by using a variety of commercial figures and converting them by changing parts and adding extra details.

military career that can be recreated. Humor and fictitious characters can also be worked into fascinating little dioramas. Who among us, who were involved in the unpleasantness with Hitler, did not love Bill Mauldin's "Willie and Joe"? The adventures of these two characters alone would furnish many ideas for humorous dioramas.

Small dioramas are usually displayed in cabinets, on tables, shelves, on the mantel or almost any place throughout the house or apartment. Their small size makes them welcome in any room as a color spot, a conversation piece, and to add interest to the room. Since they are portable, it is imperative that they be built on a sturdy base. If the scene is to contain just one of two figures without trees or other tall scenery, a piece of wood an eighth of an inch thick, providing the base is no longer than about 6 inches by 2½ inches, will be sturdy enough to support the diorama. Pieces of wood like those used for venetian blinds make good bases for small dioramas. Naturally, the diorama will look much better and be more acceptable in the room if you make the base from thicker wood and finish the edges with paint or stain and varnish. A very satisfactory base can be made from a deep picture frame such as those sold in hobby stores and artists' supply shops. Select a frame of the desired size which has high sides that are formed in graceful curves or angles; then turn the frame upside down and cut a piece of flat wood that will fit into the recess of the frame where the picture would normally go. Cement or nail the wood into the frame and then finish the outside of the frame with stain and varnish; this will give you an attractive and sturdy base for your diorama that most certainly has a professional flair.

Before fastening the figures to the base, study their positions carefully and be sure that the action and story you are going to portray will not be hidden by any scenic effects you need to complete the picture. When placement of the figures is decided upon, fasten them securely to the base. It is a good idea that, in addition to cement, you drill holes in the bases of the figures and

A striking historical diorama constructed by Robert Johnson, its realism dramatized by such things as the broken limber, overturned barrel, and patches of bushes made from liken.

fasten them with small wood screws or small nails. The figures should be fastened in place first, because when scenery is added you can bring the earth up over the bases of the figures, which will give the effect of standing on their own feet without the aid of the usual flat bases.

Among the purists, there is naturally the feeling that nothing looks more like earth than earth, nothing more like rock than rock. These are undeniable facts, but effect and results are what we are after and in many cases other materials are just as realistic looking in their final form and in many cases much easier to work with. Should the scenery on your diorama consist only of the ground the figures are standing on, texture can be obtained with a variety of artificial grasses and sands sold in model railroad and hobby stores. You can also use sawdust or wood chips and, if you like, real earth, and maybe even a small stone or two. There are a great variety of adhesives that may be used to hold the scenery in place; clear

95

Photo by Johnson
Closeup views of the broken limber and casualties in a Civil War engagement. Noteworthy are the realistic grass, hoof prints, ruts in the road, broken wheel, chains, and straps.

varnish, wood glue, model airplane cement, or any of the hundreds of commercial adhesives that are on the market. The only important thing is to have something that will hold the material you use onto the base permanently. One of the best adhesives for scenic work is "Sodium Silicate" commonly known as "Water Glass," and if you live in a rural area you may know it as "Egg Preservative". This may be bought in any drug store and the druggist will know what you are talking about by any of its three names. Beside its many qualities for scenic work, it also has the advantage of being inexpensive. To fasten the scenic material to the base, paint a heavy coat of adhesive on the base coming up over the bases of the figures and then sprinkle the material on the adhesive and allow to dry; after this it is only a matter of painting the scenery, which will be explained later.

The ground is seldom perfectly level and as your dioramas grow in size you will most certainly want to work high spots and gullies into the base so that the overall effect will be more natural. The materials to build up scenery contours are almost unlimited and experience alone will help you select the material you favor. Some of the materials used are plaster of paris, patching plaster, asbestos flakes, furnace cement, as well as a variety of mixtures carried by many hobby stores. Each has its advantages and disadvantages and you alone must be the judge. There are, however, two mixtures that have found general favor among diorama makers and either one may be just what you are looking for. The first is

In this head-on closeup of a Civil War battle scene the realistic poses and expressive faces of the figures, and the battle litter along the road — which includes canteens, hats, artillery, and the lifelike wooden fence — are exceptionally vivid.

"papier mâché," the old standard material which is not only light in weight but hard and strong and takes paint well. Papier mâché is prepared in this manner: old newspaper is first dampened and then torn into tiny bits which are dropped into a pan of hot water; the pieces after soaking are torn into even smaller pieces and rubbed between the hands until the pulp is very fine and no bits of newspaper can be seen. The pulp is then put into a cloth and squeezed to remove as much water as possible. A large amount of pulp may be made and stored in a covered container for future use. However, do not add paste to the mixture until you are ready to use it, because paste becomes moldy in a short time when not used. You may use wall paper paste or any type of paste that is prepared with water. Add one part of prepared paste to two parts of the pulp and mix thoroughly; this makes a mixture that is very easy to apply in making scenery. Another favorite mixture is asbestos flakes, which may be purchased at hardware stores, or plaster of paris and water glass (sodium silicate). The three materials are mixed together until a smooth thick mixture is obtained, this mixture will cling to framework and can be molded well. It also dries hard and strong and is easily painted.

Naturally, you must have a framework on which to put whatever plaster or pulp mixture you use and the general practice is to make this from wire screen. If the diorama is very large, fine chicken wire can be used; but if the diorama is small, window screen wire is more satisfactory. With small wood blocks set up a frame for the rises in the terrain; be sure that the blocks are fastened securely to the base of the diorama. Over this framework tack the screen which will give the mixture something to cling to. With a small trowel, a knife or your hands, work the mixture into the screen so that it hooks through the wire, and then continue to model the terrain to suit your fancy; allow the material to dry before painting.

Beside the hills and ravines, there are also such things as trees, stumps, bushes and rocks that will supply more interest to the picture. Rocks may be small stones ce-

An incident in the American Revolution shown in diorama by John Scheid.

mented in place or they may be modeled from the mixture used to form the basic scenery, and then painted. Bushes and small trees may be made from twigs you have gathered, or they too may be modeled to suit their particular role in the diorama. You may purchase trees already made in the average model shop to serve the purpose, but if only one or two trees are needed it is better to build a scale model tree, taking the same care with the details that you did with the figures in the diorama. In building a tree you must first make an armature or skeleton for the trunk and branches; this is made from soft iron wire. Start with several long pieces of wire forming first the uppermost branches of the tree; with more pieces of wire proceed to form other branches of the tree, winding the wire around and down the trunk as the branches meet the tree, and this will automatically thicken the trunk in a very natural manner. Let end of the wire extend beyond the base of the trunk and twist these into roots, some of which should be inserted in holes in the diorama base to hold the tree upright and others to form exposed roots on the ground. If you are depicting a winter scene where no leaves are on the trees, proceed to cover the wire with any modeling compound such as self-hardening clay, plaster mixture, or even any of the plastic metals. Bark texture can be worked into the trunk with a sharp instrument and burls can be modeled very realistically. In the case of a tree having foliage, the same procedure is used except that pieces of lichen are fastened to the ends of the branches; this can be done by twisting the ends of the wire branches in the lichen. Lichen is a moss that can be purchased in a variety of colors from any store selling model supplies. Besides the above use, it is also ideal for making bushes, hedges and other scenic effects. The leaf effect on the trees can be made even more realistic by applying a thin adhesive such as water glass to the lichen and then sprinkling the lichen with sawdust colored to the type of leaves you desire; after the adhesive dries shake the loose sawdust from the tree. Trees are of a great variety of shapes, and you will do well to study pictures of real live trees just as carefully as you do figures before modeling them.

Tree stumps can be modeled or cut from tree branches to the size you desire; you will even find that the knots in boards can be knocked out to make exceptionally good stumps for your dioramas. Stone fences can be modeled from clay or even built up with real stone, or you can cut the fence from soft wood such as balsa, making indentations to indicate stone with a pointed instrument; brick can be modeled in the same manner. Wood or rail fences are easily made from twigs or pieces of split wood. In fact, you can reproduce any scenic effect with effort and imagination.

Just as in the completion of the individual figure, the pièce de résistance in diorama making is the painting, for here the skill of your modeling and layout will be given life and brought out in all its glory. But before starting to paint you must observe and study nature, either in real life or in colored photographs and paintings, because not all grass and leaves are green, nor is all

Closeup view of the French party in the illustration of "Friend or Foe."

earth just brown, nor all rocks gray. The earth, the sky, water and foliage are a rainbow of color and shades, and it is the proper placement of colors that bring out the life-like quality you are seeking.

The type of paint to use is up to you; it may be casein, flo-paque, oil colors or even show-card paint. The important thing is that it must not be glossy when dry. You will no doubt have better success with tube oil colors because they are easy to mix, and an inexpensive set will contain a variety of colors to produce all the shades you will need. Another thing to remember in painting scenery is that nothing looks bright and new; for a long, long time the hills, trees and rocks have been exposed to dust and weather. Not only do the sun and sky reflect and cause a variety of shades in the trees, rocks and grass, but also you will find that there is just a slight yellowish brown tint in nature. This dusty tint added to the gray of rocks or trunks of trees makes them spring into life, and the same thing holds true of all other parts of your diorama. It is said that this yellowish hue in nature is the color of earth, the dust of which is ever present in the air. Fact or fiction, the important thing is that the tint is present in nature, and when it is added to your paints it tones down the brilliant colors and makes them much more

101

Friend or Foe? Chippewa Indians make a surprise visit to a French exploring party near Sault Ste. Marie. The figures, which are two and one-eighth inches tall, are cast from lead by Theodore Haskell; the scenery and background were designed by Dorothy Barnard. This diorama, on display at the Michigan Historical Museum at Lansing, Michigan, shows three types important in early Michigan history — the priest, the soldier and the voyageur.

life-like. In oil colors raw umber is the shade that should be used to give the tint to your colors, but remember just a hint will do the trick.

As in painting a military figure, start painting the parts of your scenery that will be overlapped by other colors. For example; start with the rocks. In rocks there are a great variety of shades depending on the type, such as limestone, granite, or sandstone, and the colors may be a great variety of shades of gray, red, brown, blue, or yellow. A rock has anything but a painted look in nature and a natural effect is what you will desire; instead of painting the rocks, stain them so that the color penetrates and gives your simulated rocks the effect of having color the whole way through, just as in the real thing. This is done by thinning your paint down to where it is just a wash, and applying it to the rock formations with a large brush allowing it to soak into the plaster; continue with coats of wash until the shade you desire is obtained. Apply the wash generously and allow it to run into the crevices, and the varied densities of color will make the rocks more realistic.

Painting the balance of the landscape is carried on in much the same manner. The important thing is to remember the great variety of shades and colors in nature; earth runs in every shade from gray to black and from light red to deep brown, and grass may be seen in a variety of shades from very pale greens to rich dark shades that are almost olive. As you observe nature and study colored illustrations, you will also note that it is rare indeed to see a great expanse of solid green grass; instead there are many spaces of earth colors and it is important to reproduce these in your scenes. When painting landscapes, you will find it invaluable to have some colored illustrations of rural scenes to help guide you in colors and shades.

The type of thinner you use will naturally depend on the type of paint being used; turpentine for tube oils, water for casein or show-card color, and dio-sol for flopaque. A very handy mixing tray can be had by using cup cake tins; a different color in each compartment will give you the colors within easy reach without the danger of knocking over open bottles. Apply colors to the landscape freely; allow the various shades to blend and the results will be most pleasing. You will find that several thin coats of paint are more realistic in landscape painting than one heavy coat.

It is possible that you have a spare barn, a vacant exhibition hall, a big empty basement, or maybe a fair sized room that no one is using, and you decide to pitch the whole battle of Waterloo or Gettysburg in miniature. All of the foregoing ideas and methods will work out for your project with the exception of the base, because the dioramas mentioned previously are small portable ones built on flat bases. The project you have in mind certainly isn't portable and tables will have to be built to support it. The larger diorama base should not be flat-top tables but rather open framework ones supported on legs that will bring the top about waist high to the average man. A sturdy framework can be built from 2 x 2 wood for the legs and 1 x 4 wood for the frames. You can nail the open top tables if you like, but they will be more sturdy and also have the advantage of dismantling easily (should the occasion arise) if you take time to assemble them with wood screws or nuts and bolts. Before putting in the cross braces, plot your terrain on paper by laying out where various roads and level sections will be. By doing this you will be able to insert curved pieces or odd shaped pieces of wood to support the level surfaces. Since the rest of the top remains open you may form the supporting screen (which will hold the plaster) into deep gullies, and you may also place supports above the tabletop to support the high ground, giving you an advantage in realism over the flat-top table.

The larger sized diorama also introduces other features that are not normally found in the small portable scenes — rivers and streams and backdrops. There are a variety of ways to model streams. First you can use real water, which gets messy and is not at all recommended; then there is of course the old mirror trick which usually ends up looking like just what it is — a mirror. Streams, however, can be modeled very effectively, as any other part of the landscape. First lay out the bed of the stream in the width and direction desired. No doubt the stream will be shallow, so model the earth, undergrowth, and stones that would be on the bed of a stream, and paint them in their natural colors. However you must bear in mind that water reflects the things around it such as sky and trees, taking on the tints of the surrounding objects. Therefore, add to the colors of the stream bed a wash of bluish green. The watery look may then be added by giving the stream bed a coat of glaze or varnish to make it shine, or you may use clear cellophane to cover the bed of the stream, which will give a very realistic effect with the colors showing through. Remember to bring the banks of the stream down into the water in some places and out over it to show undercuts where the water has worn it away. Naturally, if the stream is to be very shallow, the colors of the bed will be brighter; the deeper the stream, the lighter the colors on the bed. Here and there a dull rock jutting up through the cellophane or glaze will add to the effectiveness of your handiwork.

When you make your large diorama, one thought is going to flash into your mind as a great revelation: small figures behind the standard sized ones to give the effect of distance. If you don't think of it, some bright-eyed visitor viewing your efforts is certainly going to offer the suggestion as a helpful bit of sage advice. But, unless you are prepared to go into hours of study, mathematics, color values, and shadows, you had better push the idea behind you just as you would Satan. There is more to creating an illusion of distance than making things smaller in the background. Each component part of the whole scene must diminish, not only proportionally in size, but in density of color and angle of the base. Colors are more brilliant in the foreground and detail is sharper; as you move into the middle area the colors and details become lighter and less distinct, and naturally in the background colors and details blend into soft flowing lines. This is the very stuff of the illusion of distance, and if it is not followed with accuracy and skill the diorama will have the affect of giants in the foreground being supported by midgets in the rear. The height of the diorama and the position of the viewer would also have an affect on the illusion you would be trying to create.

You can observe these conditions by walking outdoors and looking up the street and imagining lines and angles from your point of observation to the horizon. You will find that your eyes will be on a level with the horizon, whether you are standing on a high or low level, and that the sides of the street come closer together as they near the horizon. The buildings also condense, but not only do they become smaller, they also fit roughly into a long triangle with the apex in the distance. The people on the street also fit into the imaginary triangles and grow smaller and less distinct in coloring and detail as they go into the distance. You will note that although the street may be level the people appear to be standing or walking higher than you are.

If you have never seen an artist at work, you have seen movies or cartoons of them and have noticed that from time to time they hold a brush or pencil up to eye level, run their finger up and down to get a measurement, and then transfer the measurement to their canvass or paper. The canvas or piece of paper the artist is working on could be compared to a piece of glass held in front of your diorama. The points where the light rays pass through the glass would form the picture anyone looking at your diorama would see. The viewer's eye would be the apex of a series of triangles passing through the glass to the various items on the diorama. For example, lines from the head and feet of a foreground figure would pass through the glass at one position and the lines from a figure of the same size and on the same level, but in the middle of the diorama, these lines would pass through the glass not only closer together than those of the foreground figure but the one from the feet would be higher on the glass. This same condition would exist with various items in various positions on your diorama; this explains why the people on the street seem to be standing higher in the distance, although they are on your level. This also explains why you should think twice before you go into perspective with figures on your dioramas.

The scenes you are going to set up in your large dioramas really won't need a variation in sizes to gain perspective; you will no doubt have scale distances between the various figures and installations in the scene, so they will automatically fall into the proper perspective, no matter from what angle they are viewed. The only time there would be a real need for a variety of sizes of figures to gain perspective would be in a diorama or shadow box that is very narrow and yet shows a deep battle field.

You should have a backdrop or continuation of your scene painted on the wall so that your scene doesn't drop off into nothingness. Here perspective is important, and the time put into good planning and good painting will add immeasurably to the effect of your whole project. Remember that the horizon on the backdrop should be in line with the eye of the viewer (you will have to strike a happy average on this, because everyone who sees your work isn't going to be the same height). If you are going to paint figures or buildings into the background, they must fall into proper perspective with figures and houses in the foreground, and remember to make their coloring lighter and their details less distinct than those of foreground objects. Another important factor to keep in mind is how light is going to fall on your display. The lights used in the room will naturally cause the objects on your diorama to cast shadows; it would look odd for all objects in the foreground to cast shadows to one side and all objects on the background to cast them on the other side. So, while painting the background have all the lights that will be used turned on and study the shadows cast by the figures; then duplicate their positions on the backdrop.

Do not bring the back of the diorama up directly to the backdrop and hope to continue painting a road or other objects in perspective on the backdrop. Put a break of shrubbery, a stone fence, or some other scenery between the meeting points. For example, a road would curve in behind a stone fence on the diorama and then reappear in perspective on the backdrop.

Hundreds of books have been written on perspective and the study of one will be of particular value in the making of backdrops, and, if you must go into varied sized figures to gain perspective, it will be impossible to do a creditable job without a complete understanding of the subject.

CHAPTER **6**

Converting Commercial Figures

Converting is a term used in the military miniature fraternity to describe the revamping of an inexpensive commercial figure into a fine detailed example of a particular person or soldier of a regiment with all the correct equipment and uniform colors. Not only military miniature hobbyists, but all persons interested in the creative hobbies have converted inexpensive commercial items to improve their appearance and increase their use. In some cases this period of conversion is just a stepping stone for the hobbyist on his way to the creating of his own original figures, and in other cases the collector becomes so proficient in the conversion of commercial figures that he devotes his entire collection to superb little masterpieces which he has rebuilt from inexpensive toy soldier sets.

To explain just why a person becomes a military miniature enthusiast is impossible because there are many underlying reasons that draw people to these brightly colored little figures. It may be memory of playing with toy soldiers as a child, it may be caused by a visit to a historic battlefield or museum, or interest may be aroused by a motion picture, a television show or maybe the reading of a historical novel. The miniature fan's original interest may have been aroused through contact with collectors who had already found the hobby to be a source of fun and relaxation. No matter how the collector first noted little soldiers, the experience was not unlike a boy-discovers-girls episode. First he notices they are around, the more he sees them the more interesting and desirable they become; casual contacts and curiosity develop into enthusiasm, and all of a sudden — POW! — he's in love. Sometimes the first choice is the right one and he is happy for the remainder of his days; maybe the first choice wasn't what he expected, so he either tries to change the original or he attempts an entirely different type. But once the bug has bit, it's rare indeed for the victim to give up all interest. Usually he keeps on until he has found what he is looking for. True, there are those who develop a liking for a variety of types, but this often leads to confusion and great expense, which the average person would rather avoid.

Department stores, hobby stores and miniature dealers carry sets of toy soldiers that are very inexpensive. The painting of the usual inexpensive set of soldiers is, in most cases, a gaudy business. Although the color may be correct, it is only natural in order to keep the selling price down that too much effort can't be put into careful painting of details. In order to cover the figures with one quick coat, a heavy enamel paint is used, which naturally covers up some of the details of the casting underneath. In most cases, if you remove the heavy coat of paint you will find that the figures have been cast in superbly de-tailed molds. These soldiers, just as they come from the box, are interesting in themselves, and there are many collectors who have built up collections numbering in the thousands (from these inexpensive soldiers), which represent nearly all the armies of the world. This type of soldier is also favored by the war-game enthusiast who likes to do a little shooting with his game. The larger percentage of military miniature collectors had their first experience with soldiers of this type. The natural trend

Two good examples of converting an inexpensive figure by Colonel John B. Shriver and Dr. William C. Grant, Jr. The figure with the standard, which was converted by John Shriver, underwent no basic changes in the original casting other than removing the toy paint, adding pipe-cleaner plumes to the helmet and then painting in authentic colors and design. The figure of King Richard the Lionhearted underwent a number of operations before painting. Dr. Grant removed the standard, changed the position of the arms and added a cape, from toothpaste tubes, along with a number of pieces of arms equipment. The helmet and face were remodeled with plastic metal, and chain mail sections were roughened to give the proper texture.

of a person after obtaining a few miniatures is to become interested in research and discussion of military costume and history, which leads him to haunt libraries, book and print shops in quest of information about his new avocation. As his knowledge increases and the traditions and parts of the various uniforms become more familiar to him, the mass-painted toy soldiers lose a certain amount of their appeal and he plans ways to improve their appearance, which leads him into the fascinating field of converting.

Each portion of a military uniform has a reason for being there and many times the reason is steeped in history and tradition. The proper placement and painting of these various parts of the uniform naturally add a great deal to the figure as well as a great pride and satisfaction for the hobbyist in his creating ability. In many cases, the casting under the heavy coat of paint is sufficiently detailed to give you an opportunity to create an interesting and life-like miniature just by removing the original paint and repainting the figure carefully in proper details and colors, without making any changes or additions in the original casting. Any good paint and varnish remover which may be purchased at a paint or hardware store is in most cases excellent for removing the paint from metal soldiers. It would be well to select a non-inflammable mixture and pay strict attention to any warnings that are printed on the container in reference to ventilation and handling of the liquid. Put plenty of newspaper on the table where you are going to work because paint remover will spot anything it comes in contact with, and be sure there is nothing nearby that may be damaged by accidentally splashing the solution on it. Pour sufficient paint remover to cover the figure or figures into a container and place the figures in it. Give the paint remover a chance to work on the paint for a few minutes and then, while the figures remain in the solution, brush over the figures with an ordinary inexpensive paint brush until most of the paint has been removed. Then take the figure from the solution and finish cleaning the paint out of the details with a stiffer brush (such as an old tooth brush) dipped into the solution. Wash any remaining paint remover from the figure with soap and water and then proceed with the painting of the figure as explained in the chapter on painting.

Most of the lower priced sets of toy soldiers offered today are made in foreign countries, with Great Britain no doubt being the most prominent in the field. It is understandable, then, that most of the soldiers in these inexpensive sets are of foreign troops, much to the bewilderment of the novice collector who has his heart set on troops of the United States. However, an important fact that the newcomer to the hobby overlooks is that uniforms of various countries, even of the United States, are similar during any particular period of history, and with a little effort and research the collector can convert many of the figures depicting foreign troops into those of the United States. The uniforms of the United States have been just as picturesque and colorful as those of any country in the world, with coats, jackets and trousers of almost every color and description topped with hats, caps and helmets, including tricorne, tarbucket, spiked helmet, bearskin, kepi, turban, chapeau, sun helmet and many, many others; so that with a little research and ingenuity the collector can select any number of metal figures of foreign armies and convert them to those of the United States.

The important tools you will need for conversion operations are a jeweler's saw or a razor saw, a sharp modeler's knife, a small soldering iron and some small files. These tools are, naturally, in addition to your paints and brushes. You may use an ordinary hack saw if you like, but the jeweler or razor saw has a much thinner blade and you do not lose as much metal when making cuts in the figures. After research has been completed, it is possible that you may find an inexpensive casting that is in the position you desire and in some cases only a little filing on the headgear or maybe the addition of some small details will suffice to prepare the casting for painting in the period and regiment you desire. Many figures in the inexpensive sets have movable arms which, because of the manner in which they are fastened to the body, make a very unsightly joint, which you will want to eliminate in order to give your finished figure a smooth professional look. There are several ways of covering this joint; the easiest method is to cement the arm into position with liquid solder, and then filling in with the liquid solder until the joint is smooth. When using liquid solder, which may be purchased in most hardware stores and hobby stores, follow the directions carefully and allow the material enough time to dry before painting. Liquid solder

112

as well as any of the well known fast-drying cements will make a good solid joint if directions are followed and sufficient time is allowed for the cement to set before painting or touching the parts being cemented. Liquid solder has a heavier body than cements, which is why the liquid solder may also be used as a filler around the joints. However, many collectors prefer the cement for holding the parts together, and make a filler, which becomes very hard and holds well, by mixing cement and molding powder or plaster of paris into a paste and filling in around the joints. Both methods when properly used give satisfactory results. Keep in mind that any liquid will shrink slightly as it dries, so build up the filler slightly above the joints being filled and you can trim off the excess when it has dried.

Texture and detail are the two important things you are seeking beside accuracy of uniform, and both liquid solder or a mixture of molding powder and cement will help you gain satisfactory results with a little patience and practice. Feathers and furs play an important part in uniforms of many regiments. The big bearskins of the British Guards and Napoleon's Grenadiers, along with the feathers of the Scotch bonnets and the plumes worn by the regiments of many countries, including the United States, all have a particular texture that can be reproduced on miniatures, which needless to say will add a great deal to the finished figure. A surprisingly realistic fur effect can be obtained by covering the portion of the figure that is to represent fur with a coat of liquid solder or the mixture of cement and molding powder, give it a few moments to stiffen and then with a tooth pick pull the mixture out from the figure in tiny peaks. When the portion of the figure has been covered with a rough furry texture, allow the mixture to dry completely before painting. Feather plumes and beards, mustaches and even hair can be built up in this manner. The application of a thin layer of cement before placing the mixture on the figure will give it greater holding power; however, you will find that the detail added will hold up very well

113

Four views of an outstanding job of figure converting by William E. Greer. The inexpensive casting used as a basic figure is shown in each photograph with the paint removed. In converting a figure, Mr. Greer first selects a figure-casting nearest the pose desired; the casting is cleaned and then solder is used liberally to fill holes, holding the pieces together and providing a base for build-up work. Plastic metal is then used to build-up the form. In this particular figure the pack, canteen, busby and plume were all constructed of plastic metal, as were the legs and body, entailing a bit of sculpture work in addition. The musket was fashioned with scrap lead and wire, while the blanket roll, straps, and other accouterments were made from old tooth-paste tubes. The completed figure is a private of the 21st Foot (1815). Information for the uniform was taken from *Regiments and Uniforms of the British Army* by Barnes.

after it has been painted. The same materials may also be used to add many other details found on uniforms, such as hat cords, epaulets, lace, frogs, aiguillettes, sashes, insignia and many other fine details in much the same manner as you would decorate a cake. Naturally, the placement of small details requires a degree of skill and patience, which will come to you with practice once you know how to go about it; and here is how you go about it. If you are a medical man and have access to a hypodermic needle, you have a very fine tool for decorating by just filling the needle with one of the above mixtures and pressing it onto the figure in the desired designs. Since hypodermic needles are not available to everyone, many hobby stores carry a tool known as a glue or cement gun which is a syringe type apparatus having a small opening; and this tool will do a satisfactory job. However, many collectors prefer to make their own decorators, because they are inexpensive, easy to make, and have the advantage that after use you can throw them away and make another when you need it. The best material to use in making a decorator is either heavy wax paper or heavy aluminum foil. You may use parchment paper or any other heavy paper if you like, but wax paper or aluminum is far more satisfactory for the job, with the aluminum foil being the best for the task at hand. There is no set size; however, a square of paper or foil about five or six inches square will make a convenient size decorator that is small and easy to hold. First fold the material in half diagonally (point to point); then take one of the corners on the folded edge and bring it up to the point on the open side of the triangle and press flat; next take the opposite corner on the folded edge and bring the paper or foil up and around the first folds. This will form the cone into which you will place the decorating material. Press the edges between your fingers, and the cone will open with a straight top on the front of the cone and a high peaked top to the back; place the decorating material in the cone, fold the peaked side over the front, and roll the cone down toward the point as you would a tube of tooth

115

paste. Punch a very tiny pin hole in the point of the cone and, as you wind the cone down, a very fine beading of material will be ejected. Some collectors prefer to punch the tiny hole before filling the cone; this is, however, something you must decide for yourself after trials. Don't expect perfect results with your first trial; it will take practice to control the flow of material and it will be well for you to practice on a piece of metal or glass before trying it on a miniature. Beside the materials described above for raised decorating, there are a number of plastic materials offered by various hobby and handicraft stores. In the event you are using oil colors to paint your miniatures, you may also apply heavy oil pigments to your figures by this method. Needless to say, experimenting is an exciting and important part of the hobby, and a constant search for new materials and methods will add much to your enjoyment.

Miniatures from the lower priced sets, for economy reasons, often have belts and straps painted on the figures, and much of the detail that extends away from the main figures, such as horses' reins, hat cords on Hussars, etc., is of necessity cast heavy and tight against the miniature. Substantial improvement can be made to the figures by filing away these heavy details and replacing them with details that are smaller and more in scale with the figure and not cast tight against the figure. The stranded wire from ordinary electric light cord is excellent for details of this type, and after you have stripped away the insulation and untwisted the strands of wire, you can take any number of strands and retwist them to the thickness you desire. Special effect for details such as aiguillettes may be obtained by plaiting a few strands into a cord. Tassels are easily formed by tying a knot in a number of wire strands and fanning out the ends, which may then be trimmed with an ordinary pair of scissors or shears. Small gauge brass, copper, phosphorous bronze or soft iron wire can be used with good results for horse reins and for straps on scabbards, sabretasches and other equipment. The wire may be made flat by hammering it on a smooth metal surface. If you wish you may soften the wire by holding it over a low flame until it is red hot before hammering; however, be careful that you don't let it get too hot or the wire will disintegrate. Hammering will have a tendency to harden the wire again and, should it become too stiff to serve your purpose, you may remove the temper by carefully reheating it after you have flattened it. Phosphorous bronze wire, which you may obtain from most hardware and hobby stores, is by far the best wire for adding details. It works easily and if you are soldered. The small gauge round wire can be used also not only solders well but does not transport the heat along the entire wire as readily as many other metals do. This makes it easier to solder one end of the wire, without a previous solder joint on the other end becoming unsoldered. The small gauge round wire can be used also to form small rings which, when properly placed in conjunction with the wire straps, add a great deal to the effect; tiny spurs, stirrups, and many other details will suggest themselves once you study the figure to be converted. In attaching the various wire detail to the figure, it will simplify your work to first drill a tiny hole in the figure so that the wire can be inserted, giving it a solid foundation to hold to, in addition to the cement. A variety of small drills and a pin vise will take care of this operation with little effort.

Another material important in the conversion of commercial figures is a thin piece of metal to make belts, shoulder straps, saddle blankets, coats and capes, hat brims and cap visors, as well as glove gauntlets and many other parts of the uniform and equipment. The almost universal source of supply for thin workable metal among experienced figure makers is old shaving cream and tooth paste tubes that have been smoothed out and the printing removed. The metal from tubes is easy to cut to size and shape, is easily attached to the basic figure and will hold its shape after being formed on the miniature. A variety of hat types, as well as caps and helmets, can be formed by filing away brims on the headgear of the original

117

The Archbishop of York, the Archbishop of Canterbury with his Deacon, and the Dean of Westminster. This group of 54mm two and one-eighth inch figures was made by Henry H. Morriss and is particularly arresting because toy figures of a farm woman were used as the basic pieces for conversion. Capes and other clothing were cut from thin strips of lead and jewels were taken from inexpensive jewelry.

Religious groups such as this add a great deal of interest to coronation scenes, religious pageants and the like

figure and rebuilding the crown with either filler material, solder, or plastic metal to the desired shape, and then making the brim or visor from thin metal which may be bent into position to form tricorne, chapeau, campaign, or any other type of headgear. The way to make belts and slings is obvious, since it is only a matter of cutting strips of the metal to the desired width and attaching them in the proper places. To make longer tails on a coat or collars and lapels: first file a flat indentation (as deep as the metal is thick) into the figure at the point where the extension is to be attached. Cut the metal to the desired size and shape and cement or solder the extension into the flat indentation you have filed into the figure. This will give a smooth joint and make the addition look like a part of the original casting after you have filled any cracks and painted the figure. The free end of the extension may be swung away from the figure in a very realistic manner.

Cements of various types serve well for all purposes of conversion which is concerned mainly with the repainting and the additions of details. However, as you advance into conversions that require major operations you will find that solder will be a more satisfactory bonding material, as well as a perfect medium for building up parts you wish to reshape. You may be one who is laboring under a fear of not being able to use a soldering iron, which is nonsense. You can master any tool by learning its capacities, following a few simple rules, and keeping in mind that skill comes only with practice. The best solder for miniature work is wire solder, which is about $\frac{3}{32}$ of an inch in diameter and can be purchased wound on a variety of size spools. You should avoid the various core solders, such as acid and rosin core. Core solders have a tendency to leave a residue in and around the joints which will often cause corrosion. Solder is a combination of tin and lead and the most common mixture is 50% tin and 50% lead. There are other mixtures you can use that will melt faster because they have a larger proportion of tin in the mixture; you will, however, find these higher tin mixtures better for building up portions and filling than for joining parts, for, although the softer solder melts faster and makes a smooth joint, the joints will not stand as much stress as those made with regular solder. Some collectors spot solder the parts together with 50-50 solder, and then fill in with the solder having a higher tin content; while others spot solder the parts and fill with plastic metals or other filling compounds, which gives them the strength of a solder joint and the ease of filling and smoothing with a cold compound. In order that the soldered joint will hold, the metals being joined (at the point of contact) must be as hot as the molten solder; therefore you must select a soldering iron that will get hot enough to do the job. One of the greatest failings of the novice is to expect a big glob of half melted solder to hold pieces together. An important fact to remember is that you can't make good solder joints unless the parts to be joined are clean; so with a small file or emory cloth make the parts bright and free from all grease, dirt and paint. You will also need a small can of soldering paste. This is a compound that looks something like heavy grease, and you can

119

apply a thin coating of it to the parts to be soldered with a small stick or stiff brush. Cleanliness is the watchword throughout the soldering operation and a clean bright point on your iron is important. Making the point of the iron bright is what is known as "tinning" the iron. If you have an iron that is dirty and pitted, you can rehabilitate it back into the society of respectable irons in this manner: first file all the pits out of the point; now plug the iron into an electrical outlet to heat; when the iron has heated dip the point into the can of soldering paste. If the paste gives a hiss, the iron is usually hot enough. Touch some wire solder to the point of the iron and then take a folded rag (plenty of folds so you don't burn yourself) and spread the solder over the point forming the tin; if the iron gets too hot the tinned surface will turn a dirty brown and should be wiped clean immediately. There are soldering irons that have thermostatic controls which maintain proper heat for the job at hand, and the investment in an iron of this type will more than repay you in ease of soldering. Even if you have a brand new iron, you must "tin" it before soldering in order to do good work. When you have finished using your iron, always allow it to cool slowly and be sure to wipe the point with the folded cloth to keep it tinned and in good condition.

Solder gets mighty hot so you won't be able to hold parts with your fingers while joining them; it is a good idea to place the figure in a small vise or clamp. The part to be joined to the main figure may be held with pliers or it may be held in place with thin wire, being sure that the wire holding the part does not come in contact with the solder. Since you will most likely be working with lead castings, you must work quickly so that you do not melt the parts being soldered, using the minimum amount of heat necessary to make the joint. There are several ways to keep down the temperature of the castings (away from the joints being made). One is to hold a big pair of pliers around the casting, and another is to wrap the figure (away from the joint — remember hot lead and water don't mix) with a damp cloth. Most inexpensive military miniatures are hollow cast and naturally melt much faster than solid ones. You can overcome this a great deal by drilling a hole in the casting and stuffing it full of fine steel wool (0000 is fine) which will take up a great amount of the heat. Just close the hole with solder and leave the steel wool inside the finished figure. In the case of soldering arms, it is sometimes of advantage to file a small V channel around the section to be soldered so that plenty of solder can get next to the parts. In attaching flat pieces of metal, such as coat tails, you may "tin" the figure and the piece of metal (as you tinned the point of the iron) so that when the two parts are placed together and the iron is applied, the solder will melt and the two pieces will be joined. This is known as "sweat soldering". When making a simple solder joint just touch the solder against the point of the well tinned soldering iron and enough solder will adhere to the point of the iron to do the job. However, when building up a section or part of the figure, hold the coil of solder in one hand and melt it against the iron which is being held to the part being built up. Work quickly when building up portions so that the original casting isn't melted and do not worry about smoothing the excess with the iron; final shaping can be done with a model knife or small files. Follow these few simple rules and you will have more successful soldering: (1) Keep the work to be soldered clean and covered with a coat of soldering paste, or flux; (2) Keep soldering iron clean, well tinned and hot enough to melt the solder; (3) Work quickly.

Once you have mastered the soldering iron, your scope of conversion possibilities will have expanded tremendously. You will be able to perform major operations on individual figures and combine parts from several figures into one, with results that are impossible to obtain with cements. Before doing too much converting that requires

121

removing and adding parts, you should get yourself a "Heck" box. This may be any sturdy box about the size of a cigar box. You place all the leftover parts from figures you have robbed to convert another figure, along with all the little bits of metal, chain, and doodads you will be picking up to use someday. The only trouble is that, usually, when the day comes around and the perfect use for the gadget has been found, it's a case of the collector searching high and low, either mumbling to himself or screaming to high heaven, "WHERE THE HECK IS IT?" Needless to say, there are some collectors whose language is a little on the robust side and their names for these boxes are quite varied.

When you perform major operations in order to change the position of a figure, always keep in mind the limitations of movement in the various parts of the body as explained in the chapter on Anatomy and Drapery. In order to complete particular dioramas, you will probably want to change some castings into sitting, kneeling or a number of other positions. True the arms and legs of many figures can be bent into position by warming them and then slowly bending. However, this method often ends up with arms and legs looking very much like pieces of bent rubber hose, because the knees and elbows are curved rather than being sharply defined as they should be. A more realistic position change can be made by cutting the figure at the joint to be angled and then soldering or cementing it, after the member has been placed in the proper position. Another advantage of this method is that you do not hazard the possibility of breaking the part as you would in ordinary bending. For example: the case of an arm which you want to bend at the elbow. The elbow is a hinged joint that bends in one direction and when it is bent the back of the arm must still measure the same length, or you will have a deformed soldier on your hands. With a jeweler's or razor saw cut a wedge out of the inside of the arm directly in front of the elbow, leaving the metal joined at the elbow; the size

This action group of an officer of the 7th Hussars and a French grenadier fighting, was the handiwork of Gordon Dumbleton by converting inexpensive figures. The mounted figure was made from a British life guard by cutting off the horse's head at the neck and of the man at the waist, and soldering them into the desired position. The busby and plume were built up with plastic material, the jacket was added from old tooth-paste tube metal, and various other details, such as reins and sabretache, were made from wire and thin metal. The foot figure was fashioned from a life guard of the Danish army in a similar manner.

of the wedge depends on how far you want to bend the arm. It is now only a matter of bending the arm until the cut edges meet and then soldering or cementing in place. In changing the positions of the leg, the operation is the same in reference to the knees. However, in the case of the hip, you will want to maintain the length of the upper leg; so cut from the back of the figure leaving the metal joined in front of the hip and bend the leg into position. Fill the hole left in the back and under the hip with filling compound or solder. These same methods may be used in changing the positions of horses and other animals. It is a good policy before cutting into a figure to study pictures of people or horses in the position you are trying to obtain, and it will even help to make rough sketches of the various positions you are going to make. Striking the pose yourself before a mirror will also help.

Heads may be cut from one figure and put on another and bodies may be cut at the waist and changed to another position. Should you find difficulty in soldering or cementing parts in place on hollow castings, cut a plug from soft wood which will fit snugly into each part and insert inside the respective parts. This will support the parts while you cement or solder them in place.

Although much of the foregoing has made reference to hollow cast figures, this doesn't mean there are not commercial figures cast solid. You will find some of the inexpensive figures cast solid, and all of the super detailed figures made by the well known figure makers are solid castings. Many of the figure makers of today were military miniature hobbyists and, knowing the likes and pitfalls of the collectors, have designed their products to give the collector figures and parts in the manner that suits their varied tastes. The hobby stores and military miniature dealers can today supply castings just as they come from the mold and the collector can finish the castings, and himself assemble and paint the figure, or he may buy the castings filed and assembled so that only painting remains. Some dealers even stock various parts such as heads, swords, and muskets for the collector who wants to obtain detailed parts of the proper period to complete his figures. Converting figures is without a doubt one of the most fascinating facets of the hobby and will add many happy hours to your hobby, as well as many new and exciting figures that are your very own creation.

This group of German flag bearers, converted and painted by Colonel John S. Shriver, are from a basic commercial casting. The heads have been either filed or built-up with plastic metal to the proper headgear, the flags, as well as straps and belts on the figures, from toothpaste tubes.

CHAPTER 7

Making an Original Model

The methods and materials used to make an original model depend on the final results desired by the collector. An original model may be made so that duplicates may be cast in plaster molds, or the original may be created as a one-of-a-kind figure, not intended to be duplicated in molds. You must decide before starting your figure which type of model you desire, because in making a model for plaster mold reproduction there are a number of precautions that should be taken in order to eliminate mold-making problems. Because most collectors look forward to the thrill of casting original figures from molds they have created, and because in some cases there is an advantage to using cast parts in the creation of a one-of-a-kind figure, making an original for reproduction in a plaster mold will be discussed first.

Before starting actual work on the original figure, research and planning are mandatory if your final figure is to come up to your expectations. The chapters on Anatomy and Drapery and Source Material will prove of particular value in planning and making your original. Although you may have an ideal mental picture of the figure you are going to make, you should get it on paper

From left to right; Major of the Jersey Blues (1776), Captain of the United States Marines (1812), Troy Citizens Corps (1836-47) and the New York 7th Regiment (1847). These finely detailed lead models, of the standard two and one-eighth inch size, are originals made by Eugene B. Custer.

before starting. This does not mean that your drawings of the proposed figure should be works of art in themselves; in fact, even if you draw only straight lines in the proper proportions to indicate the pose and action of the figure, they will serve the purpose of a more elaborate drawing. These preparatory sketches are invaluable because they will help you to eliminate many of the pitfalls you would otherwise encounter, such as bad proportions in arms and legs, as well as unnatural positions. One of the most conspicuous errors made by the amateur is to ignore completely the center of gravity, making their figures take unnatural poses that in real life would throw the figure flat on his face or posterior. Although it is certainly not necessary, an inexpensive manikin which you can purchase at any art supply store will also be of help. Manikins are usually made of wood or metal, hinged at all the joints such as knees, hips, and elbows, so that you may make them assume any action pose of the human body. By making the manikin assume the position of your proposed figure, you will find it very helpful to refer to while modeling your original.

The original figure may be modeled or carved out of almost any material: wood, wax, soap, modeling clay, plastic metal, plastic wood, and lead. In using materials

127

First City Troop of Philadelphia made by Dorothy and Bill Harle, a husband and wife team. The figures are originals and everything from the research through clay models, casting and final painting with Flo-Paque and oils is done by this team.

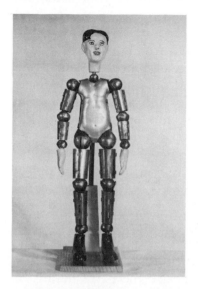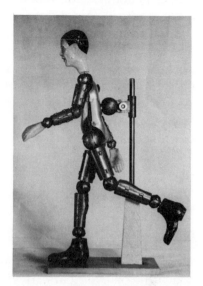

A mannikin will help you to decide on figure positions. These figures come in a great variety of sizes and prices and may be purchased from any art supply store; some are made of wood, others of metal, and still others in fully-formed rubber with wire cores so that they may be bent to the positions desired.

like wood and soap, one first sketches the outline of the figure on the block of material, and the excess material is carved away in the usual wood carving or whittling manner. In the case of the soft or plastic materials such as clay and wax, the figure is usually built around a skeleton known as an armature. Armatures are made of any wire that is soft enough to bend easily with the fingers, yet firm enough to stand upright and support the modeling material after it is formed into position. In making the armature, be careful to make accurate measurements, so that the finished figure will be in proper proportion. Form a loop for the head and twist a number of strands of wire together for torso, legs, and arms. Allow an extra amount of wire at the feet so that the finished armature may be fastened to a block of wood or metal for support while the figure is being modeled; the extra wire and base can easily be removed when the model is completed. When the position of your armature is satisfactory, run a coat of solder over the wire to bind the wire and make the frame sturdier. In the case of an armature for a horse or other item which has a suspended portion between the legs, fasten a support of wire from the temporary base to the middle of the suspended section; this will keep the weight of the modeling material from causing a sag. After the modeling material has hardened, the support wire may be removed.

The important thing to remember in modeling a figure for reproduction in a mold is to avoid undercuts, unless you want to go into multiple piece molds instead of the simple two piece ones which are more practical. An undercut is any place where wet plaster may hook under and make it impossible to remove the figure from the mold, such as a cupped hand, a turned back lapel or coat tail, or even ears. If you desire the extra details of deep undercuts, they are easily cut or scribed into the lead casting after it has left the mold. In the original model all detail lines and modeling must be clean and straight into the figure; in fact, it will be an advantage to allow a very slight outward taper along all raised portions such as lapels. This taper is known as draft and insures easy removal of the casting from the mold.

It stands to reason that the simpler your original model is, the easier it is to make your mold, and by the same token, the less complicated the mold the longer its life, because there will be less chance of breakage in removing castings. For this reason most experienced figure makers model their figures in several pieces, or cut a complete figure into sections before making a mold. The figure is usually divided in this manner: the trunk and legs in one section, the head in another and the arms in another. Besides the advantages gained in making the mold you also gain the advantage of having parts which may be assembled in such a manner that different poses may be obtained from the same mold. For example: the head may be placed so that the figure is looking to either side, or up, or down; the arms may be placed in a number of

From left to right; a Hessian grenadier of the American Revolution period, a Union drummer from the American Civil War, and an Old Guard from Napoleon's army. These four and one-half inch figures were made by Richard T. Brady. In making his miniatures, Mr. Brady first casts a nude form on which he models clothing with modeling clay; from this model plaster molds are made and the clothed figure is cast in lead. Straps, hat brims, and other details are cut from thin metal and fastened to the figures. Mr. Brady has a flair for utilizing unusual items; for example, in this case an ordinary wooden spool does duty as a drum and a piece of pipe cleaner makes an excellent plume for the Old Guard's hat.

positions which will add a great amount of variety and interest to your collection. Equipment such as belts, cartridge boxes, and swords may be modeled and cast on the torso section or they may be cast separately and fastened to the body in the same manner as the head and arms. Separate castings are the most interesting to work with because, just as you gain variety with the placement of heads and arms, so you can vary the positions of the various pieces of equipment and weapons to make a more natural looking group of figures.

Artillery pieces and other machines of war may be modeled and cast in very much the same manner as figures, and here too it is to your advantage to break the

Members of Wayne's Legion, the King's Own Scottish Borderers and a Saxon axe fighter, are reproduced by three original models in standard 54mm size by William F. Imrie. The grass on the base of the Wayne's Legion figure greatly increases its realism.

model down into a number of separate parts before making the mold for casting. Wood and metal are by far the best materials to use in making patterns or originals for artillery pieces. Cannon barrels may be carved or better still turned to shape on a lathe. If a lathe is not available, a satisfactory job of rounding and finishing a barrel may be done in this manner. First carve a piece of wood as near to shape as you can, leaving an extension of wood at one end so that it may be held. Screw a fair sized wood screw into the end of the wood extension left on the cannon barrel, taking care to center the screw; allow at least three quarters of an inch of the screw to extend out of the wood and then cut the head of the screw off with a saw. Now clamp an ordinary hand drill into a sturdy vise which has been fastened to a solid table and place the end of the screw into the chuck of the drill; insert the screw end deep enough to bring the wood firmly against the end of the chuck when it is tightened. While turning the handle of the drill, shape and finish the barrel with small files and sand paper. Of course, you can turn with one hand and finish with the other, but it's better to call in a helper to furnish the power for the drill while you give your full attention to the modeling. Besides, allowing other members of your family to help create a model is an excellent way to indoctrinate them into the hobby, and to encourage them to become your allies. Of course, you may insert the screw into the muzzle of the cannon if you prefer, so that the ball or any other extension at the breech may be more easily shaped and formed. Beside rounding gun barrels, this method of turning may be used for forming and finishing a great number of small parts from wood and metal.

Carriages and other parts for the cannon may be made of wood for each individual model, or these too may be cast after patterns are made. The best material to use in making patterns or original models for gun carriages and wagon parts is wood. The wood may be of any available kind, even balsa which is obtainable in a variety of sizes at any model store. Details such as bolts and plates may be made from shim brass or paper and small pins

You can turn many small parts of your figures from wood or soft metal by clamping a drill in a vise. Chuck the material to be fashioned into the drill and get someone to turn the handle while you shape the material with files and sandpaper.

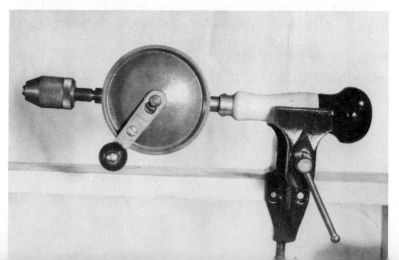

This figure was carved from wood and is seven inches tall to top of plume. A very realistic effect in equipment was obtained by making belts, sword knots, chin strap, aiguillette, epaulettes, spurs, and other accouterments from wire.

or nails, keeping in mind that all parts of the original that are to be cast must be tight and have no undercuts. Rivet bands and strips may also be made from thin metal or paper; rivets may be indicated on the metal bands by tapping lightly with a center punch on the underneath of the metal before attaching to the main portion of the model. Effective rivet detail may be obtained even on paper bands by running a cog wheel from an old clock along the underside of the paper strip. This same method may also be used on very thin metals and makes very realistic evenly spaced rivet detail.

If you have selected modeling clay of the everplastic type, wax, or metal to make your original model, there is no special preparation for making your plaster molds, because all of the above repel water and the plaster shouldn't stick to the model. However, if you use wood, self-hardening clay, plastic wood, or any other porous material for the model, you must prepare the work so that it repels water, before it is placed in plaster. This may be done in a number of ways, but no doubt the simplest is to give the model several coats of shellac or

134

varnish followed by wax or a very thin application of oil. When your pattern figure or model has been checked and prepared to repel moisture, proceed by carefully following the instructions set forth in the chapter entitled, "Making Molds and Casting".

In making one-of-a-kind originals the materials and methods are unlimited, because here you do not have to contend with the problems involved in making a pattern that must conform to certain rules so that it may be recast. In this type of figure you may combine a great variety of materials and obtain unusual and realistic effects with no worries about undercuts and textures. Wood, cloth, plastic metal, pipe cleaners, string, solder, plaster of paris, papier-mache and an unlimited variety of other materials can be incorporated in constructing successful models of this type. Only a very few of the various methods employed are described here, but they will no doubt suggest many other procedures and materials that you may employ in making an original.

A favorite method used by the greater number of collectors is to dress a nude figure in uniform by cementing or soldering clothing which has been cut from sheet lead or an old toothpaste tube to the nude form. Needless to say this makes a very fascinating and realistic model because all the little belts, the jacket, vest, hat and

Three and one-quarter inch figure of Sussex Light Dragoon (Virginia State Cavalry—1861) made by A. W. "Ed" Saunders. Mr. Saunders makes his original figures by first casting a nude in spread-eagle fashion; the nude is then put into the desired position and dressed with plastic material and bits of thin metal.

other pieces of clothing can be made to drape out from the figure in a most natural manner. This type of model also has that pleasing heft of an all metal figure which is greatly desired by many collectors. The nude for this type of figure may be formed or sculptured by methods set forth earlier in this chapter; one can take proportions from the chapter on anatomy and then make a plaster mold so that a number of nudes may be cast. When one makes the original nude, a natural standing position with legs apart is best; then a variety of positions may be formed before dressing. It is also an advantage to cast the little nudes in soft lead so that some minor bends can be made without cutting the figure. Nudes made in this fashion are also valuable in making figures you wish to cast in plaster molds. To dress the nude for mold making, use modeling clay, plastic metal or any other such material to build the clothing, taking care to abide by all the rules about undercuts and draft, and then proceed to make your molds in the usual manner.

Very successful and natural looking one-of-a-kind figures can also be made from very unusual things such as pipe cleaners for example. In making a pipe cleaner figure, fold the first pipe cleaner in half and, at the point where the cleaner is bent, twist a loop or roll into a nob to form the basic head. Below the head loop, the pipe cleaner is twisted together to form the torso and the remainder of the two ends form the legs. From another cleaner, cut a piece long enough to twist around the torso at the shoulders and extend out on each side to be formed into arms. Another piece of cleaner is then wound tightly around the torso to build up thickness. Naturally, the size and portliness of the figure you have in mind will govern the amount of additional winds needed. The pipe cleaners actually form an armature or skeleton, with the advantage of a heavier rough surface to which various molding materials and paints will cling. If the model is very small the entire job of filling and modeling may be done with paint. The best paint for this purpose is show card colors or tempera which may be obtained very inexpensively in a great variety of colors and shades. Since this is a water solvent paint, it flows easily and dries slowly enough for you to blend and make special effects on your model. If your model is to have a jacket which swings away from the body or a hat that has a turned up brim, cut these parts from paper or cloth and cement them in their proper places before starting to fill and paint. You should also attach any weapons, and the figure should also be fastened to the base on which it is to stand. This may be a small square of cardboard, or better still, a small square of metal, as figures made in this manner are very light and the metal will add weight in the right place.

When you have placed the various parts of the figure into their final positions, with all clothing in place and weapons securely fastened, paint the figure and clothing with a very thick coat of white show-card color. Use the heavy show-card color just as it comes from the jar and continue to apply layers of paint so that it builds up in the pipe cleaners and makes an even surface while covering the joints where the various pieces of clothing were cemented to the figure. When the pigments have been built up to your satisfaction, set the figure aside until the paint has had a chance to dry thoroughly. When the figure is dry, inspect it for any defects that may have formed in the drying process and fill them in with more white show-card color. Now when the figure has again dried, you will have a fully formed figure with intriguing drapery and a superb surface primed and ready to paint. Use regular show-card colors to paint. Since show-card colors are water soluble, after the figure is dry spray the figure with water color fixative, which may be purchased from any art supply store, and which is applied with a small mouth spray obtainable from the same source. Some collectors prefer to coat the figures with clear plastic which may be obtained in spray cans. This is an excellent protective coat, but you must be sure the show-card colors are completely dry and the spray must be applied with great care. It is strongly recommended that

Officer of the 7th Light Dragoons (1805) from a painting by Robert Dieghton. This superb, original lead soldier was created by Frank Conley, the main castings made from lead and type metal, the small parts from brass and copper. All of the parts such as the sabretache and scabbard are attached with small rings, all straps have buckles, and cinch rings are separate. The horse has shoes with nails; the saber can be removed from the hand and will fit into the scabbard. Approximately 200 separate pieces were soldered together to make the figure.

you practice spraying with plastic before attempting to apply it to your masterpiece.

Another interesting way of creating an original one-of-a-kind figure is with wrapping string and wire. In this

138

method a wire armature is first made the same as in making an original with clay or other modeling compounds. However, instead of using the plastic material, you wind string tightly around the armature to build up the various contours of the figure, winding more coils of string where the figure is heavier such as the chest and hips and fewer winds on the smaller sections such as the neck, waist, and limbs. On sections where very small build-ups are required, the strands of the string may be twisted apart, which will make the winds on the armature smaller and smoother. An application of any good model cement when the winding of the string is begun, and frequent applications while winding, will insure a tight well-bound figure. When sufficent string has been wound on the armature to form fully rounded limbs, torso, neck and head, apply more cement to any loose bits of string and then set the figure aside for a few minutes until the cement has had time to set. When the cement is dry, the figure may be bent into the position that best suits your purpose and you may then add filler, details and paint.

The string-wound armature is full of ridges which are to your advantage, because they will give the filler something to cling to. Plastic wood, plastic metal or any like substance is used as a filler, and modeling compound and is applied over the string-wound armature. Facial features and other details are formed as the filler is applied. The same as with the models made from pipe cleaners, various details such as coat tails and hat brims are made from paper, cloth or thin metal and cemented into place. The joining edges are concealed with the material used as a filler. The type of paint for finishing is purely a matter of your own choice.

Space does not permit the explanation of all the methods of making an original figure, for it is obvious that methods and materials are unlimited. Ways and means as well as results are only limited by the ingenuity of the hobbyist. Even finances, or lack of spacious working area, need not hamper your enjoyment of this fascinating phase of collecting military miniatures.

CHAPTER **8**

Painting Military Miniatures

"Paint Covers a Multitude of Sins" is an expression you have no doubt heard many times in connection with old barns, rusty tin, and even seasoned honky-tonk queens who have gone too many seasons. Paint, however, in the case of military miniatures, should not be applied in an effort to cover up frauds or slovenly workmanship, but to bring out the fine detail and beauty of the casting and the minute additional parts the hobbyist has added to it. It is only natural for the newcomer to the hobby, when his little masterpiece reaches the painting stage, to be so eager to see the miniature in all its colorful glory that he does not exert the same care with the brush that he did with the file and knife in the preparation of the figure. Consequently, figures often look as though the paint had been applied with a putty knife and, instead of the colors complementing the miniature's detail, the heavy layers of paint have destroyed it. A fine miniature is a combination of several operation: good casting, good preparation and good painting. One is just as important as the other, and the same time and effort should be given to each; so that the finished model will be everything you expected it to be.

One of the greatest pitfalls of the amateur is false economy in the selection of his brushes. Many a novice tries to paint with cheap, unsuitable brushes that would lead even the professional to frustration. Good tools that have good care are one of the greatest helps to good work, and the type of brushes used are just as important as the paint. True, good brushes cost a little more, but they prove economical in time, because a good brush that is treated with kindness is like a good friend; it becomes suited to your ways and improves with age.

The finest brushes for miniature painting are red sables. Red sable has qualities unmatched by any other hair: strength, slim body, fine points and great resilience. Not only will it come to a needle-fine point or knife-like edge, but it will also retain its full elasticity in paint. The hair is pale red in color with darker tips and comes from the tail of the kolinsky found in Siberia and China. Since the colder the climate, the paler and more elastic the hair, the finest red sable brushes are made from the Siberian kolinsky. Not all sable brushes are red sable, and the novice should exercise caution when selecting sable brushes. The Russian Sable is a good brush, but it does not have the fine points nor the elasticity of the

The pointed brush and its many qualities are well known. The show-card brush has many excellent qualities too in miniature painting because it comes to a chisel-sharp line and will hold its shape, making it especially valuable in painting stripes and small lines.

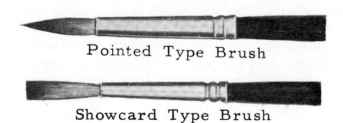

Pointed Type Brush

Showcard Type Brush

red sable. Russian sable comes from the tail of the Russian Fitch, found in southeastern Russia, Asia and Siberia. The most unsuitable sable brush for miniature painting is the black sable, which is made from the hair of the stone and baum marten and the Russian brown bear. This mixture of hair from the soft parts of the bear pelt and the tail of the marten is a deep blackish brown and has a velvet-like touch. Select your brushes with care, and they will more than repay you with smoother, better painting on your figures.

The part of the brush that is going to have much to do with the ease and satisfaction of your painting is the points. The points are the natural hair ends, and the brush makers take great caution in preserving these natural ends. After the hair is cut from the kolinsky tail (in the case of red sable) it is sized in length, tied in tiny bundles, carefully washed, and then baked in an oven for several days; particular care is taken to preserve the fine points and to remove all reversed and short hairs. The brushes are then hand cupped. The cup is a metal form, hollow inside with the exact shape of the desired style of brush. The hair is arranged in the cup and any excess is cut from the bottom of the hair, leaving the points untouched. After cupping, the hair is tied and inserted in the ferrule, then the handle is put on. You can readily see how much caution is taken to preserve the valuable points, which have so much to do with fine painting. So, never cut your brushes or you will not only cut away what you paid for, but you will ruin the brush for fine painting. Sable brushes can be bought in a great variety of sizes, from very small to very large, and three or four sizes will be sufficient to take care of your needs. Even the larger sizes will point down very small; so if your budget does not permit a selection of sizes, it will be best to buy a medium-size brush first and add the smaller and larger sizes later.

There are two shapes or styles that are best for painting miniatures; both shapes have their devotees, and by the same token, there are those who find that the use of both shapes in the painting of a figure is quite an advantage. The round pointed brush is the more common. No doubt this is because many miniature painters have not had the advantage of becoming familiar with the versatile show-card style brush. The show-card brush comes in a variety of sizes from small to large, and it is set in a round ferrule just like the round brush. However, instead of the points being arranged so that they form a point they are set so that the end of the brush is flat and looks very much like a round pointed brush that has had the point cut off. The big advantage of the show-card brush is that the brush will flatten out with paint, to cover wide areas; or, you may paint a straight wide stripe with one stroke, the width depending on the size brush you use; or, you may turn the brush to its side and draw a very thin straight line, because the brush will come to a knife edge and hold it. Once you have tried a show card brush, you will no doubt find it to be one of your favorite tools, for it is of particular value in painting stripes on trousers, etc.

Taking care of your brushes is just as important as buying good brushes, because good brushes improve with proper use. Never allow paint to dry in the hair of the brush. If you have been using oil paints, first squeeze the oil out of the brush with paper or old rags and then wash the brush in warm (not hot) water with mild soap. If you have been using enamels, dopes, or flopaque, wipe as much of the paint from the hair as you can, and then clean the brush with thinner or solvent before washing in warm soap and water. No matter what type paint you use make a special effort to remove all paint residue from the neck of the ferrule. After you wash the brush, rinse it in warm water, and then shape it between your lips. Before putting your brushes away, it will lengthen their life if you will apply vaseline to the hair, and if you are going to store them for any length of time, place some moth preventative with them, because moths find them very tasty.

There are several types of paint popular in the painting of miniatures; tube oil colors, enamels, model airplane

143

dope and flo-paque paint. The various types of paint used, however, are almost unlimited, including casein, silk screen paint, and others. Silk screen paint is well adapted to miniature painting with its wide variety of colors. Its greatest drawback is the fact that it must be purchased in large quantity and, unless a group of figure painters pool their funds in purchasing the variety of colors, one collector would be pushed out of house and home with cans of paint. Selection of the type of paint is a matter of taste, since there are advocates for each type and each has a sound reason for his devotion.

In the United States, probably the most widely used paint for military miniatures is flo-paque. Flo-paque is a trade name, but like many trade names it has become more or less a part of the language of the miniature makers' fraternity, and it can be purchased in small quantities from most hobby stores and miniature dealers. As the name implies, it is an easy flowing opaque paint that dries to a natural flat finish that is very life-like. The colors are strong and all colors may be intermixed to obtain almost any desired shade. Since the finish is without gloss, flesh and cloth clothing of the painted miniatures have a very natural look, and when portions that should shine, such as belts and boots, are given a coat of glaze or varnish over the flo-paque, the contrast in the finished model is very striking. This paint will dry in two to five minutes and is waterproof, washable, and sunfast and will not crack, peel or chip. Even greater durability can be obtained by baking, which is a very simple process and may be done with an infra-red light (obtainable from any drug store), or in the kitchen oven. If you use the infra-red bulb, place the miniature after painting about six or eight inches from the bulb and allow it to bake for approximately twenty or thirty minutes. To bake the paint in the kitchen oven, place the figure in the oven for the same length of time at not more than two hundred and seventy-five degrees. Flo-paque should be used just as it comes from the bottle; after stirring or shaking until it is of uniform consistency,

What a little paint and research will do are illustrated in these two figures which have been repainted with no changes in the toy-soldier casting. The right-hand figure in each photograph shows the toy soldier with its heavy coat of enamel, just as it was purchased. The left-hand pieces show the same figures after the heavy paint was removed and they were painted with Flo-Paque colors.

apply with a brush. It may be thinned with dio-sol (thinner) for use with a pen to add very fine detail. Dark colors may be used with a pen just as they come from the bottle; medium colors should be thinned with 25 drops of dio-sol to ½ ounce of paint, and the light colors should be thinned with 50 drops of dio-sol to the half ounce for best results.

Oil color is an old and honorable medium of painting and when it is properly applied to military miniatures, the finished figures have a matchless quality. Oils are favored by miniature artists who do portrait figures (of particular persons) and desire fine facial expressions. Oil colors may be purchased in small tubes from any art supply store and most hobby and military miniature dealers. The oil color comes from the tube in a heavy paste, which you thin with turpentine to the consistency you desire; most miniature painters squeeze a bit of oil color on a piece of glass or small dish and then add turpentine with their brush as it is needed. The only drawback with oil is that it takes quite a long time to dry; you can, however, speed up the drying process by adding a few drops of Japan Dryer, which may be obtained where you purchased the oils. The slow drying is more than compensated for by the special effects obtainable with oils, which are very hard to get with the faster drying paints. When oil colors are blended right on the figure, it is easier to obtain facial details and shading; oils may also be applied slightly heavier when painting hair and mustaches, and actual texture can be obtained with your brush which will make these parts stand out in relief. Fur hats, collars, knapsacks and many other parts of the miniature that would be improved by a furry texture can be painted with oils, and then stippled with the brush while pulling the paint out from the figure. The oil should be applied rather heavily for these fur parts, and naturally it is going to take the paint longer to dry, but the effect is well worth the wait. Oils are especially effective in the painting of horses, not only because of the ease in shading, but also because you can work texture into the horses' hair by allowing your brush strokes to show slightly in sweeping strokes that follow the contours of the animal. Oil color has the distinct advantage of smoothness or texture, whichever you desire; you may work the oil to a smooth surface that will show no brush strokes, or you may work it into rough textures that will remain when the paint has dried. Many collectors combine oil colors and flo-paque in painting their miniatures; they paint faces and hair, with oil, and clothing with flo-paque. Since the flo-paque dries quickly, the models may be handled even though the oils on the face are still wet.

Model Airplane Dope can be obtained from any model shop in small inexpensive bottles. This is a very fast drying gloss paint and may be had in a great variety of colors. Most collectors do not care for this type of paint because of the high gloss or shine; however, it is good to touch up the lower priced soldiers that come painted in a shiny finish. Since plastics have spread so widely in the model field, enamels have become familiar to the miniature maker. Beside the old familiar cans of enamel, you may now obtain small inexpensive jars of enamel that have been packaged expressly for the model maker. Enamel, like dope, has a gloss, but instead of drying quickly like the dope, it is very slow drying. Its big advantage is the even flowing quality and smooth finish obtainable, and the fact that it is safe on plastics. Paints such as flo-paque and model airplane dope will disintegrate most plastics. Types and brands of paints are unlimited; only the four most popular with miniature painters have been explained. You may find any one or combination of the above to suit your needs, or you may develop another medium more to your liking; the important thing is always to keep seeking and experimenting to improve your talents.

Before you start to paint, get all the things you will need together — your brushes, thinner (proper type for medium you are going to use) a flat piece of glass for mixing, and some soft rags to wipe your brushes. Be sure your figure is clean and free from oil or any foreign matter that will interfere with the paint; if you are going to use flo-paque colors wash the figure with dio-sol before painting. You will also find that by giving the figure a few minute's bath in vinegar the paint will adhere much better. The reason for this is the mild acid action of the vinegar will etch a microscopic tooth on the surface of the metal, giving the paint something extra to take hold of. Be sure to clean all the vinegar off the figure before painting. Holding a figure by the small base while painting sometimes gets tiring to the fingers; you may, however, avoid this cramping by cementing the figure on a block of wood, which will be much easier to hold, or on the end of a tongue depresser such as the doctor uses. These may be obtained at your local drug store. Be sure to give the cement time to dry between the base of the figure and the wood before painting. When your painting is finished it will be a simple matter to remove the wood holder and smooth up the base, so the figure will stand level.

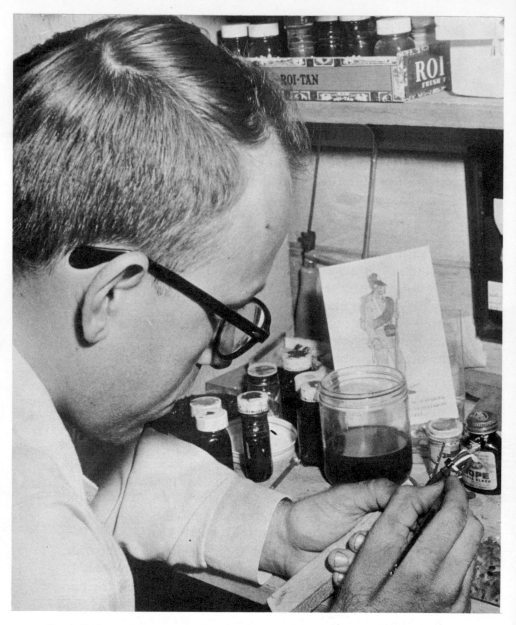

Frank Conley, well known collector and maker of miniatures, demonstrates how the painting of a small figure is made much easier by fastening it to a piece of wood. The wooden block forms a handle for the figure and it can easily be removed after the paint is dry.

After you are sure your figure is good and clean, give it a coat of white paint; this should be a good even coat but not heavy enough to cover the details in the metal figure. Allow this primer coat of white to dry before applying color. The undercoat or primer of white will not only give the colored paints something to cling to, but will also make one coat of color more brilliant. When applying the colors to your figure, proceed in the same order that the clothing would be put on. For example, first apply the flesh to face and hands; then paint the shirt and trousers before proceeding with the coat. Always paint the parts that overlap another last; in this manner the latter items painted will show a nice clean line where they overlap the previously painted portion of the figure. Complete all the large masses of color before starting to paint the small details, such as the facial features, equipment, lace and other small parts.

The first details to paint are the facial features and as these are probably the biggest problem to the novice, many times he has pop-eyed, pink-faced soldiers who look as though they have just been swiped across the mouth with a sharp saber. One reason for this condition is that color has a tendency to intensify on small objects, and especially on models. Reds are much redder, dark blues become almost black, and black is really black, and this illusion is true with all shades. No one could have lips so red as those made with plain red paint unless he was bleeding. Eyes, besides looking popped, often have a strange appearance because the miniature artist hasn't bothered to find out what eyes look like. It will be to your advantage to study illustrations of faces in magazines, and also to study methods used by professional figure painters; but the very best method is to study your own face in a mirror. Note that when you look straight ahead or to the right or left the eyelids always cover or touch a portion of the iris of the eye. Now widen your eyes and, when the iris is not touched by the eyelids, you are pop-eyed, and that is exactly why your figures look pop-eyed — the eyelids don't touch the iris or color part

149

of the eyes. Combine wide eyes with the dark intensified colors most amateurs use and your results are anything but what you are seeking — especially if the eyes are set in a pink face with blood red lips. Painting a good face like all painting is a purely mechanical operation once you have learned to observe and know what you are about. Here is a procedure that will give perfect results after a little practice.

If you have followed the previous instructions, the face and neck of the figure have already been given a coat of flesh-colored paint and all the clothing has been painted. First take a brush of white paint and fill in the section where the eye sockets will be; don't worry about trying to shape eyes, just get that particular area covered with white. Some painters like a faint tint of blue in the whites of the eye; so if you too want the bluish tint mix just a hint of blue in your white paint before applying. If the figure is to look straight ahead, paint the center of the eye directly in the middle of the white spots; naturally if the figure is to be looking to the right or left, the center of the eyes will be painted to give the direction of view. If you have problems in making the center of the eyes small and round with a brush, you may cut a piece of wood, such as a wooden match stick, to the proper size on the end and then use it like a rubber stamp to place paint representing the eye color. Keep in mind that color intensifies when used in a small place; so use light blue or light brown when you place the color in the eye. The next operation is to paint the eyelids, which must be a very fine line or your soldier will look as if he has black eyes or a terrific hangover. This is not so hard to do as you might suspect. Examine your own eyes in a mirror, and you will see that the lower lids have a slight curve and the upper ones a higher arch to the curve; in fact, the outline formed by the eyelids looks something like a plump fish that has lost his tail. You will also notice that the distance between the eyes is the same as the length of one eye, give or take a fraction. Remember, it's the *slight* difference in features that makes the difference in people's appearances. Note also that the upper lid overlaps the lower lid on the outside corner of the eye, and that the eyelids next to the nose join by a tiny curve. Since the lower lid is over-lapped by the upper, paint the lower lid first with an arch of brown, being sure that it touches the iris of the eye which you have already painted. Don't worry how wide or ragged the outside edge of your line is, but be sure the edge that meets the iris and white of the eye is smooth and sharp. Now proceed with the upper lid in the same manner; remember that the upper and lower lids join with a little curve next to the nose, and on the outside the upper lid overlaps the lower. Also remember that the upper lid has a little more curve to the arch, and just like the lower line you have painted, the inside of the line must be smooth and touch the iris or color of the eye; the outside and width of the line are unimportant at present.

If you don't want your soldier to be a pink-faced re-cruit, you will have to tone the flesh color on the face and work in some texture and lines that will show on an old campaigner. On the piece of glass or small dish you are using for mixing, put some flesh-colored paint and add with your brush a drop or so at a time) red, brown and even yellow, mixing as you go along until the flesh tone you desire is obtained. Remember colors intensify on small objects, so don't get it too dark. The first step now is to take care of the brown line you painted around the eyes. With the flesh tone you have mixed, paint over the brown lines, leaving just a tiny fraction of the brown showing around the eyes, and you will have that fine outline that you didn't think you could paint. Right above the upper eyelid should be a fold in the skin; take some of the flesh tone and add just a hint more of red to it and draw a thin line above the eyelid. If you don't think you can make it with one thin stroke of the brush, you can always make it by the same method you used to put the thin outline around the eyes. Next come the eyebrows, which must be dark enough to show well, but

151

avoid making them too dark. Needless to say, eyes are very important in forming the final expression of your figure; therefore, besides studying your own eyes in the mirror it will help you to study the colored advertising in various magazines that show faces. The next step is to paint the mouth, and this most certainly should not be bright red. Add some more red to the flesh tone on your mixing glass and paint the mouth; remember that the lips of most men are reasonably thin, so don't paint cupid bows. If you get the mouth too big or crooked, trim it with flesh tone paint the same as you trimmed around the eyes. Now continue with the flesh tone paint over the remainder of the face and neck to give them that rugged outdoor look; bring out the color of the cheeks just a bit with the addition of a hint of red. You might emphasize the nose slightly by a touch of very light brown along the sides of the nose. The amount of character lines you want to add is up to you, and light brown mixed with flesh tone will give you about the right shade, but don't overdo the painting of lines or the effect might be different from what you expected. Avoid jet black hair; lighter shades such as browns, blonds, reds and even grays are much more effective. Where the hairline meets the sides of the face and the neck, don't make sharp smooth lines as if the hair were plastered down; a rougher hair line will give a more natural appearance.

Once you are satisfied with the face, the rest of the detail on the uniform is simply a matter of knowing what colors the various parts should be and neatly painting them in their proper places. Unfortunately, many newcomers to the hobby, after learning to paint thin straight lines, allow their new found talent to get out of hand and proceed to outline everything on their figures with dark lines. Some proper shading on clothing may add to the final effect, but masses of spidery lines can do nothing but detract from good workmanship. Besides, remember the figures usually painted are in the full round and should show details cast in the metal which will cast their own shadows. However, if you must emphasize parts such as where a vest overlaps the trousers or where the coat overlaps other clothing, use a very light bluish gray wash and come up to the edge of the coat or vest and not onto it; note that the shadow is being cast by the coat or vest. If you wish to bring out folds and wrinkles in the clothing, make the lines soft and just a tone darker than the overall paint of the particular part. Since shadows have a bluish gray cast to them the addition of a little blue to the clothing color will give a good shadow effect.

Needless to say the horse under a mounted figure or in an artillery team deserves the same care and study when painting as the human figures. In fact, there is a lot more to painting a horse than just giving him a flat coat of paint with a few splashes of white on his fetlocks and forehead. Unfortunately, many city dwellers don't get a chance to study horses, but you can always turn to that great American Institution, "magazine advertising" and find scores of horses pictured in color. Your city library too is a fertile field for horse research, and also for military history. The horse is a beautiful, colorful animal, and by faithfully making an effort to reproduce the ranges of colors and tones of the horse's coat on your miniatures you will find a great deal of enjoyment.

Don't forget that old bugaboo, color intensity on small figures, because a horse painted jet black is going to be really black and a horse painted plain white is going to look like a ghost horse. By adding just a little white to your black paint, when painting a black horse, you make him a very dark charcoal shade and he will come out much nearer to what you had in mind for a black horse. When painting a white or light gray horse, remember that he has some darker shades too. Around the light horse's chest and over his hips and knees, there is usually a shade of gray that is slightly dappled, and blending these shades into your model will work wonders in creating a life-like reproduction. If you are using oil colors to paint your light horse it will be a problem of blending until you obtain the desired effect; because of the slow-drying oil, you are able to blend colors right on the horse. However, in the case of the fast-drying paints there are different methods required because the paint isn't going to wait for you to make up your mind. Here is one way to get a good dappled effect without worrying about the paint drying faster than you can work. Assuming that you have already cleaned the casting and given it a primer coat of white paint, apply another good even coat of white or light gray, whichever color horse you have in mind. Now mix a gray shade just a little darker than you have painted the horse and dry-brush this shade on the parts of the horse mentioned above, and as you found them in pictures of horses you have studied. To dry-brush doesn't mean that the brush is dry, although it is almost dry. Dry-brush is a term used for a particular type of painting, and here is how you go about it. Dip your brush, in this case a medium-sized one, in paint, and then wipe it on a piece of paper or rag until most of the paint is out of the brush, and then brush the remaining color on the item to be painted. By this system you avoid globs of paint and, because only small amounts of paint are put on the object at one time, you can feather the edges making an even blend of the darker and the lighter shade. If you must shade the uniforms on your soldiers, you will find dry-brushing a very effective method for that as well as for toning horses. After applying the dark shades to your white or gray horse in the proper places — and by the way don't overdo it with your newly found skill — you will be ready to apply the dapple spots. These can naturally be applied with a brush, but a much easier method is to twist just a bit of cotton on the end of a tooth pick or match stick which has been shaved down. Dip this tiny cotton ball into the white paint which you have spread on your mixing glass or dish, and carefully do the shaded section you have painted on the horse. Just as in the dry-brush shading, don't overdo the spots. Make them light and small and study well the pictures you have found of horses. The amount of paint on the cotton ball or tip should be about the same as a rubber stamp would pick up from a stamp pad; therefore, you may have to touch the tip on a rag to take up the excess paint before applying it to the horse.

The variety of shades and tones of browns a horse may be painted are unlimited, from light buckskins to deep reddish and golden browns, and even spotted. Obtaining the particular shade is a matter of mixing and blending until you are satisfied. Orange and brown are good colors to start with in blending colors for the medium or darker brown horse. Adding small amounts of orange to the brown will make a rich horse color, which may be toned with the addition of other colors to create a great variety of natural colors. You will note in the pictures you study that some darker horses have the spotted effect much like the white and gray horses previously mentioned; the various darker and even lighter shades may be dry-brushed on the horse. Interesting highlights or character-istics of various horses such as white legs or spots on forehead can be applied without any special instructions, and their placement will be very clear in the illustrations you have studied in various books and magazines. The mane and tail of the horse are usually darker than his overall coat, and in many cases the area around the nose and mouth is a dark grayish shade. If your horse's mouth is open, don't forget to show the teeth, and if his hoof is turned up, be sure to paint the horseshoe on the bottom; all these little details are important in adding interest to the finished figure.

Metallic colors such as gold, silver, copper, and gun-metal are all very important to the final details in mini-ature figures; however, their application should be made with a great deal of care so that they add rather than detract from the overall picture. Various metallic colors are supplied by firms packaging model airplane dopes, enamels and flo-paque colors. These are usually mellow paints that are well suited to miniature painting because they do not have the harshness of bronzing paints, which are better suited for painting radiators, pipes and wire fences. Nevertheless, you will find that unusual highlighted

155

effects can be obtained by combining the various metallic enamels and paints with the harsher or more brilliant bronzing liquids. For example; in the case of gold epaulets, paint the epaulet all over with a coat of gold dope, enamel or flo-paque and then, when the gold is dry, take a fine pointed brush and add small contour lines with the more brilliant bronzing liquid. This will add just enough sparkle to the gold to give it extra life and quality, instead of having the gaudy quality of an epaulet painted with bronzing liquid. This same system of highlighting may also be used on gold hat bands, the bullion on the ends of sashes, and the many other metallic parts of a military figure's equipment. It works equally well with silver and other shades as it does with gold. A combination of the two kinds of metallic paint is also valuable in bringing out the designs on helmet plates and belt buckles in much the same manner by painting the section first with the more mellow metallic color and then painting the design on the plate or buckle with the more brilliant bronzing liquid; this process will make just enough contrast to give a pleasing effect.

Metallic colors are very important in painting figures that wear armor, both plate and chain, and your selection of the proper shade or brilliance will have a great deal to do with the effectiveness of the finished job. Plate armor was both dull and polished, so you have a choice here in selection of the brilliant or more mellow type of paint, depending on the period and on whether the figure is wearing battle or parade armor. In the case of chain armor, this is usually shown duller than the plate armor and you will find a gun-metal shade very effective. Gun-metal may be purchased already mixed or you may mix graphite with silver paint to obtain a very effective color for chain mail armor. Graphite may be purchased in powdered form or you may easily make graphite powder by rubbing an ordinary lead pencil on sand paper. Gun-metal shades are also very effective for rifle and musket barrels as well as for sabers because, although equipment may be polished to its peak for parades, it is rare for sparkling equipment to show up in the field. Just as the combination of two types of metallic paint is of value in emphasizing the gold in epaulets, hat cords, and cap plates, combining of the two types is also valuable in bringing out the links in chain mail and other items made of iron or steel.

Needless to say, all the foregoing hints, suggestions, and instructions can do no more than supply you with fundamental information, and you will have to develop your own style of miniature painting, using the mediums most suitable to your taste. You are well aware that tastes vary; you have only to witness the advocates of modern painting and sculpture to bring this fact into focus. Your greatest teacher will be the study of the work of other miniature makers and the study of paintings and colored illustrations. The portions of what you like best, transcribed to your own miniatures, will create your own personal style of painting and this, certainly, should be the most pleasing to you.

CHAPTER 9

Making Molds and Casting

Great moments of dreams and anticipation, some of the longest hours you have ever endured, a rare and exhilarating thrill and satisfying pride — all these be yours when you make your first mold and cast your first lead soldier. The mental pictures and plans that fill your mind while you prepare your first mold, the endless hours of waiting for the mold to dry, the thrill that comes when you are ready to pour molten metal into the finished mold, and the pride that surges through you when the casting is pulled from the mold you created with your own hands are not sensations that will dull with repetition. Each time, no matter how often, you create a model and reproduce it in metal in a mold you have made, all these sensations will return.

Mold making and casting is an ancient art that has not changed in principle over the thousands of years since man first learned he could melt metal and pour it into a cavity and produce his tools, ornaments and weapons. Methods have changed and improved until today much of your comforts and pleasures are a result of the mold maker's skill, but with all the refinements in the art, the principle is still to place liquified material into molds and allow it to solidify.

In the early days of casting, when molds were made of stone, the design was cut into the stone and the molten metal poured into the open cavity. Later two piece molds were made of bronze, which naturally produced better and more elaborate castings. It is interesting to note that the lost wax process which is widely used today was well known and used back in the ancient world. No better name could ever be found for this method of casting, because that is exactly what happens in the process — the wax *is* lost. In lost wax casting the original model is made of wax and then covered with the material that is being used to make the mold. The ancient craftsman usually used clay; today plaster of paris or material of general likeness is used. After the mold is dry, it is placed over heat until the wax is melted and drains out of the mold; molten metal is then poured into the cavity, and when the metal solidifies, the mold is broken away from the casting. Thus, the wax model is lost in the process and the term "lost wax" casting. Although the model and the mold are lost, this method has the advantage of producing beautifully detailed castings which require little if

casting, circa 1800 B.C. A, B and C. Show the method of hollow wax casting. Core A made of clay, model made with wax over the clay core, mold C made by covering the wax model with clay. D is a two-piece bronze mold, E is a one-piece open mold made in stone and F is a furnace with bellows.

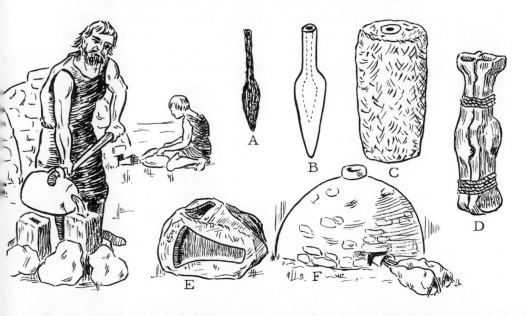

any finishing. This method also allows the casting of undercuts and details that would be impossible to obtain in a two piece mold made of plaster, clay or metal.

You have often wondered no doubt how the fine detail and undercuts were possible in the castings, made by professional military miniature makers, which you purchased from your local hobby shop or miniature figure dealer. These finely detailed castings are possible through the use of vulcanized rubber molds, which are not to be confused with molds made from liquid latex which are used to cast figurines of plaster or other material that does not require heat to liquify. In the vulcanized rubber mold method, a model made of metal is required. This model may be obtained by either the lost wax or plaster of paris method, and extra details can be engraved or soldered to the model before the vulcanized rubber mold is made.

Special equipment is required to make vulcanized rubber molds and although the machinery involved does not cost a fortune, it is far more than the average collector would care to invest to cast figures for his personal collection. The vulcanizer or machine in which the molds are made is of necessity a sturdy well-built unit, since a pressure of 15 to 25 tons is exerted in the making of the mold. The rubber used in this method of mold making is cut in discs, two being required for each mold, and it is prepared in various curing textures from soft for models with a great deal of undercut work to hard for thin flat models. The ring that holds the rubber while the mold is being made consists of a sturdy ring and a top and bottom plate all made of steel so they will not collapse under the tremendous pressure exerted to form the mold during the vulcanizing process. One of the rubber discs is placed in the mold ring, and since usually several castings are made at one time in these molds, the metal models are arranged in a circle on the bottom half of the mold rubber. A separator powder is naturally used on the models and between the mold halves to prevent the rubber from sticking to the models and the two halves of

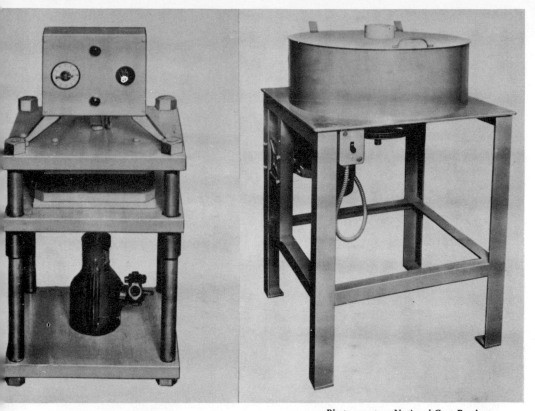

Photo courtesy National Cast Products

Rubber mold casting machinery: vulcanizer in which molds are made under fifteen tons of pressure and a centrifugal casting machine in which the castings are made.

the mold from sticking together. The top half of the rubber mold is placed in the steel ring on top of the models and the steel ring plate top is put on; then the whole works is put into the vulcanizer where pressure and heat are applied until the rubber mold is vulcanized.

There is a good reason why rubber molds are made in a disc or round form. Rubber molds are usually used in a centrifugal force casting machine. The pouring point or sprue is in the center of the circle and channels, or a spider, for the molten metal is cut from this sprue to each cavity around the mold. The casting machine spins the mold, while molten metal is being poured into the sprue. This spinning action forces the metal out into the mold cavities under pressure set up by centrifugal force, which accounts for the sharp detail in the finished casting. And

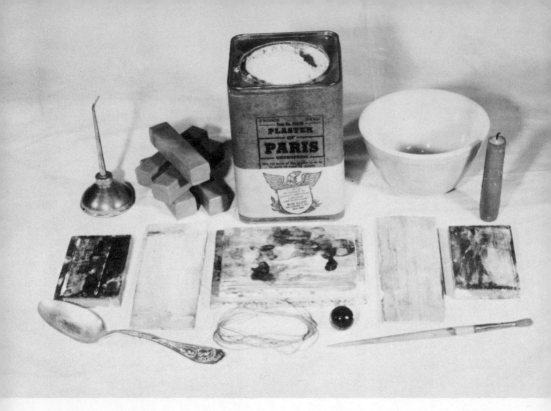

The basic things needed to make a plaster mold; plaster of paris or molding powder, modeling clay, a bo▮ in which to mix plaster, wood to construct a mold box, spoon for stirring the plaster, marble for maki▮ key marks, string for tieing up the box, brush for brushing away any foreign matter, oil for keeping mo▮ halves from sticking together (tincture of green soap may be used instead of oil) and a candle for putti▮ carbon on the mold before pouring hot metal.

since the molds are made of rubber, they are flexible enough that the finished casting, even though it has many undercuts, can be removed without damage to the mold.

There are of course various other methods of casting and there are many small details that have been left out of the foregoing descriptions of casting because of lack of space. The principal reason for the outline of casting methods is so you will better understand what happens when you follow the following instructions in making a mold of your own.

The cost of making a plaster mold in which you can cast metal soldiers is negligible; in fact, most of the items you need are common household items. You will need some wood about a quarter of an inch thick, a good sized cereal bowl or other deep dish, a large spoon, a small round sable or camel hair brush and a larger flat type camel hair brush, a small bottle of linseed oil or any light machine oil, a marble, some string, a common table knife and a sharp model knife or kitchen paring knife, a package of ever plastic clay (the kind that doesn't get hard), and a box of molding powder or plaster of paris.

First make a mold box from the wood, the wood may be thicker than ¼ inch, but shouldn't be thinner than ¼ inch because the moisture of the plaster would warp it. The following sizes may be smaller or larger if you like; however, these measurements make a very practicable size for making military miniature molds. Cut one piece of wood 6¼ inches long and 4¾ inches wide; cut another piece of wood ½ inch shorter in both length and width of the first piece, or 5¾ inches long and 4¼ inches wide. Cement or nail this piece on top of the first piece you cut, being sure the corners are good and square and the second piece is centered on the first piece. Now cut two pieces of wood 2½ inches wide and 4¼ inches long; two more pieces are then cut 2½ inches wide and 6¼ inches long. These are the sides of your mold box and will fit on top of the edge of the first piece of wood you cut, and around the second piece which you cemented or nailed to the first. Do not fasten the last four pieces of wood you cut, because these are held in place by string while the mold is being made. If you use thicker wood for your mold box, naturally you will have to change the sizes to compensate for the size of step formed where the first and second piece of wood are joined. It is important that all cuts are made good and straight and all corners are square, so your box will be solid when tied together with string.

Now examine your model figure which you are going to use as a pattern for your mold; the important thing is to find the dividing line. The dividing line is the highest line running around your figure between the front and back of your model. If you examine the lower priced lead soldiers, you will find a line of flash (flash is the metal that sometimes leaks out of the sides of a mold when castings are made) which has not been cleaned before painting. This line of flash is the dividing line on the figure. It will also help you to find the dividing line on your model by holding it up to the light, with the light directly to the back of the figure and your eye directly on the front of the figure; the exact line where the light casts a shadow around the figure is the dividing line. When you have decided just where the dividing line is on your model, draw a thin line with ink, or scribe with a sharp instrument. Ink will be better, because it is easier to see and will not mar the model. Always keep in mind that if you do not have the right dividing line, the plaster will hook over your model and you will not be able to remove it from the mold.

The next step in making your mold is to build a cradle for your model out of the plastic clay. On the bottom of your mold box (leave the sides off while you build the cradle) spread about ½ inch or so of clay, allow a little to extend over the sides because you can trim that later and make a tight fit when you tie up the sides of the box. Place your model face up on the clay bed you have made; if the model is of sturdy stuff such as metal or wood you can gently press it into the clay until the clay comes almost to the dividing line you have drawn on the model. Now take bits of clay and build up to the dividing line all around the figure; keep bringing the clay out to the edge of the box so that the figure is in a good firm base and make the clay as smooth as possible. The top of the clay need not be level but should follow the contour of the dividing line right out to the edge of the box. When you have cradled the model to your satisfaction, it is time to use the marble you have been wondering about. In each corner of the clay cradle, as far away from the model as possible, push the marble about half way into the clay making a round indentation. When you pull the marble out, smooth the edges of the clay with your finger; these indentations need not be perfect but must not have an overhang where the plaster can catch under the clay. The indentations will form the keys in the two halves of

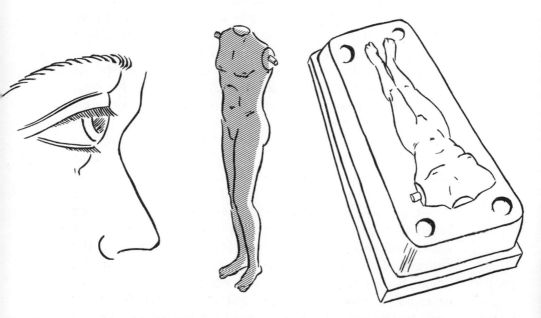

The dividing line is found by holding the model directly in line with the eye. The extreme edge of the silhouette is where the dividing line should be drawn. The model is then placed in a clay cradle, building the clay up even with the dividing line.

your mold; these keys assure the exact alignment of the two cavities when the mold halves are put together for casting.

You are now ready to pour the first half of your mold. Trim the clay that overhangs the sides of the platform on which you built the cradle; be sure to make your cuts as straight as possible, so that when the sides of the mold box are put in place around the platform they will make a tight fit. Now place the two shorter sides you cut in position on each end of the platform and the two longer sides overlapping the short ones. Start with your string at the lower half of the box you have formed and wind it tightly around the box; continue winding the string up the sides of the box until you are satisfied it is good and firm. Take small bits of clay and seal the inside corners of the box, which extend above the cradle holding your model figure. Check the model and the clay cradle to be sure you have done a neat clean job, and you might brush them lightly with the larger camel hair brush to remove any foreign matter that may have accumulated while you were assembling the mold box.

There are almost as many ways of mixing plaster as there are favorite cold remedies; everyone has his own special method and you too will no doubt develop your own special technique after making a few molds. However, if you will follow the instructions given here, you should be able to turn out a satisfactory mold on your first try. In a bowl, place what you judge to be a little more water than necessary to fill your mold box over the clay cradle and model you have prepared. It is much better to have more than you need than to find you have not mixed enough; be generous with your guess on the amount of water needed to fill the space, for you can always throw away what is not needed. Sift the plaster or molding powder through your fingers into the water until dry plaster starts to remain on the surface of the water. Do not drop handfuls of plaster into the water, because it will get lumpy and cause trouble. When you have placed the powder in the water, stir gently and continuously until the mixture starts to thicken, about eight or ten minutes. The longer you stir the mixture, the stronger the mold; however, if the plaster is not poured when it starts to thicken you will risk the danger of its forming a great number of air holes. The plaster is ready to pour into the mold box when it has reached the consistency of heavy cream. As soon as you think the plaster has reached this consistency, tap the side of the bowl sharply several times; this will bring many of the air bubbles to the top and you can quickly scoop them off before pouring the plaster. Now pour the plaster mixture into the mold box and vibrate or agitate the box, for this will cause the air bubbles to come to the surface and escape. Continue this agitation until the plaster begins to become firm and then set the box aside for about an hour until the plaster has become hard.

When you have allowed the plaster in the first half of your mold to harden, remove the sides from your mold box, pick up the plaster, and remove the clay cradle from it. Now lay the plaster, with the model figure still in it, on the bottom of the mold box and apply a coat of oil over the plaster, brushing it in well. You need not put oil on the figure. Place the sides around the platform again, tie them tight, seal the inside corners with clay, mix plaster as you did before and pour into the box, agitating it as you did when making the first half of the mold. Again set the box aside for about an hour for the plaster to harden.

Now that the second part of your mold is hard remove the box sides, separate the two halves of the mold, and remove the original model figure. If you have oiled the first half of your mold well, separation will not be a problem. If the sides do not part readily, brush some water on the parting lines and run a dull knife along the line between the two halves; you may tap the knife lightly but with care to avoid chipping the mold. Check the surface and the cavities in the mold halves for pin holes; these are tiny holes that appear when you have not been able to release all the air bubbles through agitation during the pouring of the plaster. Mix a small amount of plaster and with the small brush you will be able to touch up and fill many of these flaws. Do not bother with any holes that do not touch the figure cavity. With your model knife cut the sprue into the plaster; this is usually cut so that the lead will enter either the top or the base of the figure. The sprue is cut like the inside of a cone or funnel; in many cases it is cut into only one half of the mold, but you will have much more success if you will cut it into both halves. The point where the sprue meets the figure cavity must line up on both halves of the mold, but other than this the cuts on the two halves do not need to line up perfectly since the sprue is cut off after the figure is cast. There is no set size for the sprue, but on the average 2⅛ inch figure, cut the channel where the sprue enters the figure about ³⁄₁₆ to ¼ inch across and then taper the channel out to the edge of the plaster mold, at which point it can be up to an inch across. When you pour hot metal into your mold the air must have some place to go, so you will have to cut or scribe very small air channels from various parts of the figure cavity. Air usually builds up at the ends of extended parts such as hands. From the edge of these sections, cut a line out to the edge of the mold; always bring these lines upward (the top of your mold is the end where the sprue is located), never downward, and they must not come near the pouring sprue. These air channels should be no larger than you might scribe with an ice pick; in fact an ice pick makes a very good tool to scribe them. It is also a good idea to bevel all the outside edges of the mold; this will help prevent chipping of the mold when in use. The mold is now ready, but do not pour molten metal into it now. Moisture and molten metal are two things that don't get along well together; your mold must be completely dry before pouring your first metal casting. Drying will take, at the least, a full 24 hours. You may place the mold on a radiator or in the sun to help the drying process. You may even place it in the oven, but avoid heat above 250 degrees in drying the mold.

The mold you have made is what is known as a simple two-piece mold. You are no doubt wondering, what about horses and turned up hats and other things that could not be cast in a two piece mold. In the case of horses, you can cut the horse down the middle and make a set of two piece molds for each half; then assemble the castings. Or you may cut the legs off on either the right or left side of the model and make a two piece mold for the body and two legs; then make another mold for the two legs you have cut off. When the castings are made you can cement or solder the two leg castings onto the body casting you have made. Naturally, there are multiple piece molds; however, in a three-piece mold the insides of the horse's legs would have to be straight in order to remove the mold sections and you would lose the muscle contours on the inside of the horse's legs.

Three-piece molds are easy to make, and here is how you can make one for a figure wearing a turned-up hat. First, draw your dividing lines on your model; these will be around the figure just as they were when you drew them for a two piece mold, except that on the hat you will have two dividing lines which will follow around the edge of the turned-up hat brim. Prepare the clay cradle for your model and bring the cradle up even with the front of the hat; then fill the indentation at the crown of the hat with clay, so plaster will not hook under the model. With your marble make the usual four key indentations in the corners of the mold. Then make a key indentation in the clay directly above the hat, about half way between the model and the edge of the mold. Prepare your plaster, and pour after tying up your mold box sides. When the plaster has hardened for an hour, remove the clay from the mold half. Before pouring the second half, fill in the indentation in the hat top with clay up to the dividing line you have drawn on the back of the hat brim, and bring the clay right out to the edge of the mold in a wedge shape. Make this wedge as heavy as possible for strength, since it will be a pattern for the third piece of your mold. Make a key indentation in the wedge, oil the plaster on the first half of your mold, tie up the sides, prepare the plaster, and pour. When the plaster has hardened, separate the two halves you have made and remove the clay wedge extending from the top of the model's hat. Leave the model in the mold halves and oil the section of the halves where you removed the clay. Tie the two halves together with string, set the mold on end with the opening going down to the hat on top, prepare plaster, and pour into this opening, but be sure you fill it to the top of the mold. When the plaster hardens and you separate the parts and remove the model, you will have a three-piece mold. Cut the sprue and air channels the same as you did in the two-piece mold.

The number of pieces you incorporate into a mold is up to your own ingenuity; however, it is better to keep the mold as simple as possible and each section of the

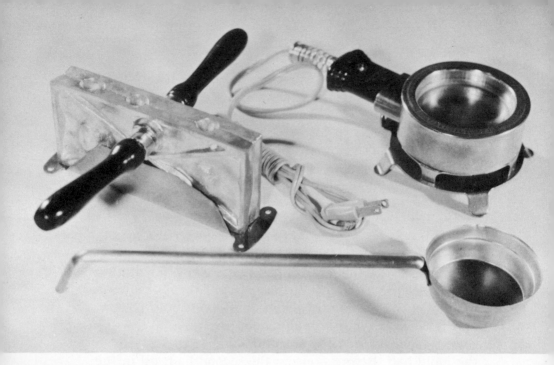

This home-casting outfit consists of a heating unit, ladle, clamp for holding molds, and wood handles to hold the two halves of the molds. Casting sets such as this one, together with a variety of metal molds, can be purchased in many hobby shops and department stores.

mold as heavy as possible, because plaster is fragile and often an ambitious undertaking in a many-pieced mold leads only to confusion for the amateur.

Now after hours of waiting and anticipation you are ready to cast the metal figure. You will need a ladle, some casting metal, a candle, some string, a pair of pliers, and naturally a method of heating the metal. Since lead melts at about 620 degrees Fahrenheit, and most mixtures of metals used for military miniatures melt around this temperature, give or take a few degrees, you can heat your metal on the gas stove or electric burner. If your hobby shop or military miniature dealer cannot supply you with casting metal or a ladle, you might try a hardware store or plumber supply house. Metal may also be obtained from dealers in non ferrous metals, which you will no doubt find listed in your telephone directory. Lead makes a very sturdy casting, but it lacks luster and sharp detail; while type metal gives you a bright sharp detailed casting, but is brittle. Just as there are many opinions on cold remedies and mixing plaster, there are many "sworn-by" mixtures of metal for casting, but the general consensus of opinion among amateur figure makers is that a mixture of about 50-50 of lead and type metal gives a sturdy well-detailed casting. The pliers, string and candle you already have — so you are ready to go.

While your metal is heating in the ladle, light your candle and hold it under the cavity of each mold section until the inside of the cavities are good and black; this deposit of carbon is needed only in the cavity of the mold. Various people use different coatings such as stove blackening and graphite; however, there is nothing easier to

Harry Barker, well-known maker and collector of military miniatures, confirms the fact that you do not need a special shop in order to follow the hobby. He is shown in his kitchen casting figures from plaster molds.

A study of this simple two-piece metal mold will be helpful in making your own plaster molds. The pouring points are seen at the top of the molds and the keys (small bumps and indentations) for holding the two halves in line.

use or that gives better results than the carbon from a candle. When your mold cavities are coated with carbon, tie the mold together with string and don't forget to use plenty. In fact, there is no need to tie the string if you wrap a lot of it around the mold, since it will have a tendency to bind itself. Naturally, you may use rubber bands; but if the hot metal spills out of the mold on to the rubber, the lady of the house is promptly going to move your little foundry outdoors. When your metal has melted you will find a scum has formed on the top. You may remove this by scooping it off with a flat stick or piece of metal. One way to test if your metal is hot enough to pour, without a temperature gauge, is to fold a piece of newspaper a few times and quickly dip it into the metal and withdraw it immediately. If the end of the paper is a nice toast brown, the metal is hot enough to pour. Pour the metal steadily into the mold sprue until the metal is even with the top; in just a few moments you will notice a crysallization action of the metal, and when the metal becomes solid at the pouring point, you can unwrap the string, open the mold, and carefully remove the lead casting. The sprue is cut off with the pliers and thrown back into the ladle to be remelted. Now is the time to check if the metal filled all portions of the mold cavity. If it did not, take your model knife and scribe small air channels from the portion of the cavity which did not fill, so that the built-up air may escape when you

172

pour the next casting. If in your eagerness to remove the first casting you broke out a section of your mold and it is in one or several large pieces, you can cement them in place in your mold, but you must allow the cemented section to dry for several hours before you coat the section with carbon and cast another figure.

Remember, plaster molds are not production molds and you can not expect to cast hundreds of figures at one time. If you will give the mold a little rest after several castings, it will last much longer. It is better to have several molds when you are casting and use them in succession; in this manner you will not burn up your molds. One method of making duplicate molds is to place a mold half in the bottom of the mold box and, after oiling it well and tying up the mold box sides, pour plaster into it. This will give you what might be called a positive of the mold half. Repeat the same operation with the other half of the mold. Then when you want to make additional molds, you can cast them from these positives, rather than building a clay cradle around an original figure.

Mold making and casting, like everything creative, requires practice. Each time you make a mold your skill will increase, but no matter how many molds you make, there will always be that thrill of creation that never dies.

CHAPTER **10**

Anatomy and Drapery

One of the most discouraging discoveries for the amateur figure maker is to realize that, after hours of uniform research, modeling, casting and careful painting, the finished figure doesn't look right. Not only in making original figures, but often in converting commercial figures to various action poses, the hobbyist is disappointed with the final product of his efforts. No doubt the principal reason for his miniatures not coming up to expectations is that, in his fervor to reproduce uniform accuracy, he overlooked the fact that the human body is built on a framework of bone that is hinged to move only in particular directions and areas. When this frame is set in motion and positions change, each component part falls into a distinct pattern; when the miniature figure maker overlooks these characteristics, his final model is going to leave something to be desired.

You are indeed a very fortunate person because every day you are surrounded by thousands of operating examples of anatomy and drapery. Keep your eyes open, in your home, on the streets, or anywhere there are people, and you will gain a great deal of knowledge that will help you to improve the positions and drapery of your little masterpieces. You own and have at your constant beck and call an operating full size model to study, your own body. If you can not convince a friend or member of your household to assume particular positions while you copy them in your miniature, strike the pose yourself before a mirror, and study the positions of your arms, legs, and balance when striking a particular action pose.

To be sure, over the years there have been rules set down by artists and sculptors for the proportions of the human body. Naturally they vary, but the movement of bones in a normal person is always in the same pattern. In the more or less accepted proportions listed here, you will find a lot of information that will improve your original figures. However, don't forget the human element — people are different. They are tall, short, thin and fat, and it will be your aptitude in combining these human qualities with the ideal proportions set forth that will determine just how natural and lifelike your miniatures will look. All too often the miniature maker makes a fetish out of his devout adherence to a definite height scale for all his creations. This unwavering dedication to height scale creates armies of one size men, which would no doubt be an ideal situation in real life; but as you have already discovered, real life soldiers are not all the same size, either in height or width. When a height for a type of figure is set, such as the popular 2⅛-inch-high size, this means the normal six-foot man standing erect without headgear is 2⅛ inches tall. You are well aware that real armies are made up of men shorter than six feet and men taller than six feet, as well as men exactly six feet tall. Your ability to make adjustments in commercial figures, and in modeling your own original figures to a variety of heights and proportions, will have a great deal to do with obtaining the natural lifelike quality you are seeking in your collection. Needless to say, it would be impossible to tell or teach you all there is to know about anatomy and drapery even in a volume much larger than this whole book; you will find many books on the subjects in your local library and book stores.

They will not only improve your figure making, but you will also find the subject extremely interesting and educational.

When you decide the proportions for the human body, the head is used as a unit of measurement. For example, what is called the ideal figure by most artists is a figure eight heads tall. From the top of the head to the chin is one head, from the chin down to the nipples of the breast is another head in length, from the nipples to the navel is another head and from the navel to the crotch is another head, making four head lengths or the middle of the figure. From the crotch to about midway of the thigh is a head length, from that point to the bottom of the knee is another head and the final two head lengths are taken up with the distance from right under the knee to the bottom of the foot. The elbows come just about in line with the navel when the arms are relaxed at the side, and the wrists fall just below the crotch or middle of the figure. The distance across the chest and upper arms, about in line with the nipples, is approximately 2⅓ head lengths, and at the waist about one head length. What beautiful specimens the men of the human race would be if they did measure up to these proportions, which they usually do not; however, following this set of measurements will make an attractive and well balanced figure. A very simple method of arriving at the sizes without going into fractions and figuring is to cut a strip of paper about ¼ inch wide and as long as the figure you are going to make. Fold the paper once in half, then repeat, folding in half two more times. When you unfold the length of paper, you will have an accurate scale divided in exactly eight parts, or the eight head lengths of your proposed figure.

Unfortunately the male figure in most cases is a little dumpier than the so called ideal proportions given above. For the purist, here are measurements nearer to the actual male figure. The first three head lengths fall about the same — the chin, the nipples and the navel; but the fourth head length falls slightly below the crotch and

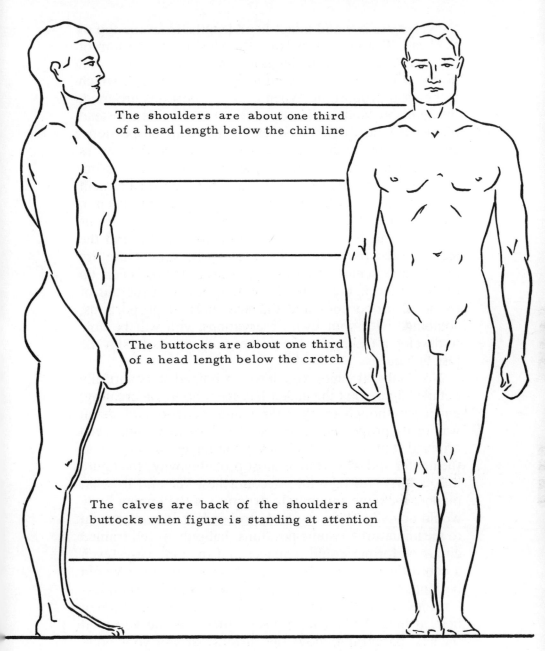

The shoulders are about one third
of a head length below the chin line

The buttocks are about one third
of a head length below the crotch

The calves are back of the shoulders and
buttocks when figure is standing at attention

A male figure divided into the ideal proportions of eight heads tall.

the knees are five and a half head lengths from the top of the head. The lower legs from the knee to the bottom of the foot are two head lengths long, making the total height of the figure 7½ head lengths instead of 8, which is the ideal proportion. When these proportions are used, the figure is about two heads wide at the shoulders instead of the 2⅓ head lengths given in the ideal proportions. However, always keep in mind that it is the differences in proportions that make people different, and it is impossible to formulate elaborate rules for the measurement and comparison of the human body. One thing to keep in mind is that the difference in the heights of various people is chiefly due to the length of the trunk, and the legs between the knee and ankle. To be sure, there are many more scales and rules of measurements, even up to the heroic figures nine heads tall, but with the aid of the ideal proportions and the near normal proportions, combined with your own observations, you will be able to develop a feeling for the proper proportions to suit the task at hand.

No doubt at times you have examined a beautifully detailed figure that the maker has spent hours on creating, and even though every button and weapon and detail was in its proper place, the soldier looked wrong, even crippled, but you couldn't lay your finger on what was the matter and why. Here is most probably why: the figure maker forgot to take into account how far and in what manner the bone and muscle structure of the human body would actually allow the body to bend. It is not unusual to see miniatures assume positions that only a well trained circus performer could manage, and in some cases even a contortionist would be put to shame, because it would be humanly impossible to strike the particular pose. As I mentioned in the opening of this chapter, the human body is hinged to move in a set pattern. While you read the next paragraph, move the various parts of your body as indicated and you will gain a better understanding than all the words and pictures in the world could convey.

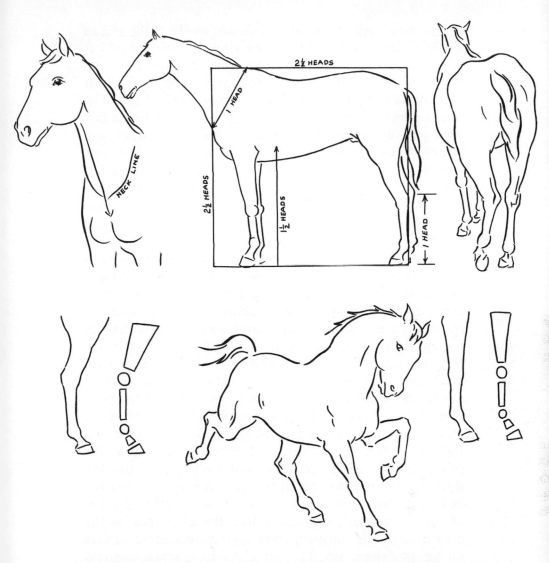

Animals also have patterns of movement. For example the neck swings from side to side and up and down from the line where the neck joins the body. The hip and ribs work much like those in the human body, swinging up and down with movement. You will observe how the hips angle when the horse is standing at rest. The leg structure can be broken down into a series of balls and blocks to help in making them bend in the right places.

Different breeds have different shaped heads, features and bodies; the study of a variety of book and magazine pictures will help a great deal in modeling your horses.

The head will move up and down, to the right and to the left, but notice that when moving to the right or left it stops about the time it gets to your shoulder line; and if you want to look to the back, you must swing your shoulder and upper part of your body to the back. The upper part of your body or chest is very much like a box with your arms hooked on in a ball joint, and when you swing your shoulder back on the right side, for instance, the left side of the box moves forward and when the left shoulder is swung back the right one goes forward. Since the arms are put on in a manner which allows several directions of movement, you can swing them straight out to the side, you can swing them out in the back, and you can swing them up over your head. However, when it comes to the elbow, the movement is more restricted and is almost confined to strictly a hinge, where the lower arm can be bent up to the shoulder from the inside of the arm only. The wrist and hand, like the shoulder has a great deal of flexibility, and does not present too much of a problem in being misplaced by the miniature maker. Each time the arm is moved in such a manner that it affects the position of the shoulder, it also affects the position of the chest box. The one end swings forward as the other goes back when the shoulder is raised; in stretching the arm overhead, one side of the box swings up as the other end swings down. This naturally places the left shoulder lower than the right when reaching above the head with the right arm or vice versa. Another portion of the framework very much like the chest box is the area around the hips; this box also moves more or less on an axis since, just like the chest box, when one end moves one way the other swings in the opposite direction. The box at the hips may remain straight forward when the chest box is swung to the right or left; however, when the chest box is tilted up or down the hip box also goes into action but in an opposite fashion. For example, if the right shoulder is swung up and the left goes down, the left hip comes up and the right hip goes down. The torso or trunk of the body may bend forward and to either

180

side but it won't bend backward, although it will arch back to a certain degree. The legs joined to the ends of the hip box will swing forward, backward and to the side; however, when you come to the knee joint, the movement is restricted — like the elbow, it bends only to the back. Keep these few simple movements in mind when you are modeling or converting figures into action positions, and you won't end up with an army of deformed soldiers.

This officer of the Jersey Blues in the American Revolution is an example of a figure which has been dressed with thin pieces of metal such as that provided by old tooth-paste tubes. The body was cast from lead; then clothing, such as waistcoat, coat, cape straps and other articles, including the hat and bow on the hair, also made from thin metal, were put on the figure. The figure was made by Tom Bauer.

Drapery, which is no more than cloth used as a covering for the nude form, like anatomy and action can best be studied by watching the people you come in contact with every day, and in making a study of the strains and folds that show up in your own clothing when you strike various poses in front of your mirror. When the figure is standing straight with arms relaxed at the sides, the upper clothing is supported by the shoulders, chest and upper back. The lower clothing is supported by the hips and buttocks. If the garments are well cut and well fitted, (but who ever heard of well fitted G.I. issue?) there will be no folds in the garments except where they may be crushed by belts. However, any movement of the body, no matter how slight, will cause folds in the garments. Each fold is governed by the position of the figure, and the proper placement of these folds on your miniature will most certainly increase the realism you are seeking.

Pull and crush are the two important factors in causing the folds or wrinkles in clothing, beside such things as belts and slings. In the case of the clothing around the belt or slings, the folds will depend on just how tight the belts are drawn and the folds will radiate from the belt very much like those in a bag with a string tied around it. The depth and number of folds depends on how closely the garment fits the body and how tightly the belt is drawn. Folds caused by pull will radiate from such points as the elbows, shoulders, knees, crotch, arm pits and supporting surfaces of the figure, while crush folds will usually be formed under the elbows and knees and around the waist when these portions of the figure are bent. If you will take a large square of cloth and hold it up by one corner, you will note it falls in a series of more or less straight folds, which start at your hand and widen out at the lower part of the cloth. Take the same piece of cloth and hold it up by two corners and the folds will radiate in sweeping arcs from your hands. The two types of folds formed in the cloth when holding it by one corner and then by two are the basic folds you will find in clothing which will be caused by the points of pull — straight folds when the clothing is being pulled at one point, and arched when pulled from more than one point. The tightness of the folds of course depends on how much strain is being exerted on the cloth. Extreme pull from several points at one time will naturally pull the arcs into almost fans of straight folds. Roll the piece of cloth loosely around a cardboard tube or round stick, and then push the cloth together from both ends; the bunching of the cloth forms crush folds. You will find these folds being formed in the clothing of any bent figure, or where movement of the figure causes the clothing to bunch. Keep in mind that clothing is very much like a series of cylinders of cloth, five in all; one cylinder for the trunk or torso, two for the legs and two for the arms; so the crush patterns on the clothing of your figure will follow those formed when you pushed the piece of cloth together on the stick or tube.

Study the patterns of folds formed in your own clothing as you flex your arms and legs before a mirror; note the folds formed at such points as the bent elbow and knee, where both pull and crush are combined. The extra effort you expend in carefully working the proper folds into the clothing of your miniature will more than repay you in the satisfaction of a job well done. True, many figure makers depend on paint to create these folds, but you are creating figures in the full round; therefore it is only natural that folds should be in full relief. If you are converting or finishing commercial castings that do not have the folds cast in them, take the time to file or carve them on the figure before painting. You will be glad you did when you place the finished piece on display.

CHAPTER 11

Source Material

There is an old, old adage that often the journey is more exciting than the arrival. This certainly holds true many times in the search for uniform information and other military knowledge, to complete a miniature or diorama. The exploration for uniform and weapon information is one of the most interesting facets of the hobby. It is often as impractical to accept one source as it is to abide by many popular beliefs that have been retold for generations with the customary additions here and deletions there. Accurate information about uniforms of the armies of Europe and the Old World is naturally abundant, because a military heritage existed there long before the forces of the United States were conceived. However, the last few decades have produced a thirst for knowledge about American uniforms and military history, which has been due in no small part to the increasing growth of making and collecting military miniatures as a hobby. Advertising men, always alert to the trends and interests of the public, have in many cases turned to the colorful military uniform as an attention-getter to sell their clients' products. The entertainment world, just as alert to the public's tastes, molds motion pictures and television shows around wars and the men who fought them. The novelist, too, has found the historical novel with dashing military heroes and exciting military incidents much to the public's liking. And military students have produced a host of volumes extolling the exploits of both heroes and rogues, from low recruit to high brass.

The entertainment world as well as the historic novelist enjoys poetic license which permits deviation from fact in order to add sparkle, and therefore inaccuracy and whimsy is to be expected. Although the student and historical writer do not enjoy poetic license, inaccuracies have a way of creeping into his works. This unfortunate situation occurs for a variety of reasons. A student will often accept the error put down by an accepted authority without seeking other opinions or checking recent information. For this reason it behooves the collector not to accept one source alone, but to delve deeply into every possible library, museum and private collection to compare and determine the worth of each student's opinion.

Although there have been distinguishable features in the clothing of soldiers since ancient times, military uniforms, as thought of today, have a history of only a few hundred years. Hannibal raised the white and crimson Spanish regiments, the Crusaders wore clothing emblazoned with crosses of distinctive colors, men of the feudal barons went into battle wearing the liveries of their masters, and mercenaries depended on scarves of distinctive colors to distinguish their allies. Men have banded together in groups to fight their enemies ever since there were men, and it is only logical that they should develop a variety of clothing or insignia to distinguish each other in the excitement of battle. The search of old manuscripts and accounts reveals many interesting examples beside the few mentioned above. It is interesting to note that what is considered to be one of the first military uniforms as we know them today is still worn in much the same pattern as originally designed. The Yeomen of the Guard, known popularly as Beefeaters, formed by Henry VII

185

during the latter part of the fifteenth century, was uniformed in the reign of Henry VIII with a costume of typical Tudor pattern with puffed and slashed sleeves and breeches with tight hose and a narrow-brimmed low-crowned hat. Through the centuries this uniform has changed very little in basic pattern and the Guard is still clothed in a red Tudor patterned uniform armed with sword and halberd.

In the latter part of the seventeenth century, several regiments were formed and with them came distinctive uniforms. From then to the present century, uniform designers have had a field day trying to outdo each other with embellishments and color. During some periods, horsemen were weighted down with silver lace and bound in tight clothing until it became an effort to swing a saber, while foot troops were poured so neatly into their uniforms that the free movements required in battle were greatly encumbered. All this makes one wonder if the idea was to scare the enemy with gaudy fantastic clothing, just as the savage paints his face, or if the array of finery was a method of encouraging the enlistment of recruits who could then strut like peacocks, flouting their plumage for the fair sex and satisfying their egos.

Research on development of most old world uniforms is greatly simplified because of records kept by monarchs and nobles through the years enumerating how many bolts of this type cloth and how much for this and that to outfit troops. These records, coupled with the paintings and prints produced to satisfy the peoples' love for the military, and the publication of strict rules and regulations for the armed forces, gives the researcher a fertile field in which to work. The uniforms of the United States, however, present a tougher row to plow for the student, not only because the United States has always been a peace-loving nation but also because in earlier years money and materials were not as plentiful to supply troops with standardized clothing and equipment as it is today. This does not mean that there were no colorful uniforms in America's history. Nothing could be further from the truth; as the country grew in wealth and power uniforms blossomed out in color and style to equal the clothing and equipment of the older nations. Unfortunately much early information has become lost, and many records are not as clear as they could be and depend a great deal on the scholars' interpretation, which naturally can lead to a variety of views. But this very lack of early information adds zeal to the quest and makes this part of the hobby even more enticing. Where shall he turn for this information is the natural question of the hobbyist, and the following leads will open many avenues of military knowledge.

National museums not only house extensive displays of uniforms but also maintain large libraries of information which is available to the public. State museums also abound in knowledge that is yours for the asking. The same applies to city and private museums which have been founded and maintained for the sole purpose of gathering and passing historic information on to the public. Many museums publish bulletins and from time to time books and pamphlets dealing with armor, uniforms and other military subjects. Public libraries are also at your service and many have set up sections devoted to prints and books on costume which naturally include military uniforms. The various historical societies throughout the nation are also a good source of information; many have museums where actual uniforms are displayed, and they all maintain collections of books, newspapers and historic records which will yield much about various regiments and their activities. Old newspapers carried not only descriptions of parades and gatherings of military units, but also advertisements for the apprehension of deserters which described their uniforms. Paintings and prints of the various museums are also valuable in your search for information. The primitive type paintings are exceptionally interesting to the scholar because what the amateur painter lacked in perspective and technique, he made up for in exacting detail, which is often eliminated by the professional.

HOSPITAL STEWARD. ORDNANCE SERGEANT. COMMISSARY SERGEANT. GREAT COAT FOR ALL ENLISTED MEN.

A page from the *Uniform of the Army of the United States, 1882* which was prepared under instructions of the Quartermaster General. A number of such books of various periods were published and many may be found in the libraries of historical societies as well as public and private libraries. Books of the same type were published on flags also. Volumes of this type go into great detail with both colored plates and line drawings of equipment and insignia. In foreign countries there have also been published books such as these; the Confederate States of America also issued one.

Residents of state capitals and the larger cities throughout the nation need go no further than the telephone directory to find the addresses of museums and historic groups, since many are located in the larger cities and seats of state government. If none are listed, a letter to your state or federal representative will most certainly be channeled to the proper agency to supply you with addresses. However, a far simpler method is to purchase a World Almanac from your local book store or news dealer. The World Almanac is inexpensive and contains names and addresses of the various museums and historic societies. You will find the directors and curators of museums as a general rule very enthusiastic and eager to help you with your study.

The United States Government Printing office publishes a number of full color prints which may be purchased at a very nominal price. Catalogs listing the various publications may be obtained by directing a letter to the Superintendent of Documents, U. S. Government Printing Office, Washington 25, D. C. Be sure to specify in your letter that you are interested in Army or Navy, because catalogs are issued on a great number of subjects.

There always have been and always will be men who enjoy soldiering. Needless to say, this enjoyment is found more in fancy uniforms and parades than battle and bloodshed. America saw the banding together of such men as early as 1638 when the Honorable Artillery Company was formed in Boston. By the middle of the following century, a variety of such groups of volunteers were formed, such as Smallwood's Maryland, The Jersey Blues, and Haslet's Delaware. In fact, it was such units that accounted for the early success of the Continental Army and it is no wonder that Washington recommended that the United States depend on such militia for defense in the new government. Volunteer companies continued to increase in numbers and colorful splendor, each trying to outdo the other in spectacular uniforms until, by the middle of the nineteenth century, almost every town boasted at least one company and some cities had hundreds. They would fall out for a parade at the drop of a hat, and rivalry between companies, encouraged by political and ancestral ties in some cities, ran high.

These volunteer soldiers who were the predecessors of today's National Guard financed themselves with little help or interest from the Federal Government, but when the nation went to war the volunteers marched off to do their duty for their government. When the Civil War broke out, the volunteer companies of both the North and the South made up a large portion of the fighting forces.

Early months saw many brilliant uniforms in the field, but as the war wore on the finery gave way to more service-able and inconspicuous clothing, although some groups continued to cling to distinctive uniforms of modified form.

Just as with the regulars of any country, the uniforms of the United States Army, Navy and Marines also changed many times in cut and color over the years, and examples of these along with pictures and text may be found in the various museums and libraries. A number of illus-trated books in full color on United States uniforms have been published under the direction of the Quartermaster General, no doubt the best known being the set of H. A. Ogden, which was published during the latter part of the nineteenth century. Containing a great number of colored plates along with regulations from the Conti-nental Army up to the time of publication, this is indeed a valuable source of information, although some students say that earlier uniforms shown are not correct. Other Quartermaster books are naturally smaller but the colored illustrations show the uniforms of the particular period from a variety of angles, with regulations and line draw-ings of insignia and other uniform details. Army Regula-tions which have been issued by the authority of the War Department lack the colorful pictures, but the text covers uniforms of the period of issue in detail, along with much other information of interest to the military student. Naturally, there are regulations for the other branches as well as for the Army. Needless to say, books of this type are not easy to come by. A stroke of luck may turn up copies in antique shops or second-hand book stores, but don't build your hopes too high. How-ever, you would do well to seek out your local museums and public libraries, because most of them have copies of some.

Probably the first set of prints on contemporary soldiers was produced from wood cuts made by a group of artists in the service of Emperor Maximilian during the early part of the sixteenth century. The first prints of American soldiers were produced in Europe near the end of the American Revolution. People who love beauty and history have always collected pictures, but it has only been since the advent of efficient reproductive processes that picture collecting could spread beyond the few who could afford the costly originals. The nineteenth century saw the woodcut develop into fine engraving and the lithograph, which brought colored illustrations within the budget of picture hungry people. Early lithographers turned out hundreds of thousands of inexpensive prints on a wide variety of subjects which were bought up as fast as they could be produced. Books rolled off the presses illustrated in brilliant color, but now inexpensive enough for almost everyone to afford. The covers of sheet music now boasted inspiring colored illustrations instead of merely type, and not the least among these works of art were uniformed soldiers on the covers of music written and dedicated to the various volunteer companies. As may be expected, sometimes the printers were a little careless in selection of colors and maybe the draftsmen were a little loose with some details, but study of these pictures, when possible, should not be overlooked in your search for uniform information.

The nineteenth century also saw the growth of another great institution — advertising. Manufacturers and merchants, seeing the impact of colored pictures on the public, soon put the magic of color to work drawing people's attention to their products through colored posters, fancy labels, beautiful boxes and, that most fascinating of all, trade cards. It is not unusual at all since the world was military conscious that many posters, labels, and cards showed soldiers in their designs. Trade cards were distributed in a variety of ways, sometimes packed in the merchandise and sometimes given by the seller, and the subject matter was on every conceivable subject, including flowers, birds, heroes, medals, daring actresses, pirates, wicked bathing beauties and, that most important subject, military uniforms. Pictures and advertising messages were printed and distributed in a great variety of

Advertising inserts such as these cards, which are to be cut out and made to stand, were very popular during the latter part of the nineteenth and early part of the twentieth century. Advertisers are again turning to the colored inserts which are to be found in a variety of products. One French firm is reenclosing fully-colored uniform cards in tins of biscuits. Inserts showing flags, presidents and uniforms have been appearing with bubble gum in the United States.

VATE. 1ST REGT. MASS V.M

ILLUST'D SWEET CAPORAL
PRIVATE. NAT. LANCERS. MASS. V.M.

ILLUST'D SWEET CAPORAL
KEGK ZOUAVES. JOHNSTOWN. N.Y. MILITIA

ILLUST'D SWEET CAPORAL
OFFICER 22ND REG. N.Y.S.M.

There are thousands of different cigarette cards on military subjects. Beside single uniforms, as above, there are battle scenes, medals, weapons, headgear types and others. Collecting cigarette cards is a hobby in itself, and like stamps, coins or any of the collecting avocations there is a great range in the cost of cigarette cards running as they do from pennies to dollars. The cards illustrated are from the famous Kinney Tobacco Company's Military Series which became, really, an encyclopedia of army uniforms; over 600 different cards were published. This series is especially sought after because of the colorful Volunteer Company uniforms of the United States.
Cigarette cards are excellent source material and fine painting guides.

sizes and on many different materials, beside paper and cardboard, including silk, felt, and leather. The ones of most interest to the military miniature collector and, fortunately, the ones that have survived the rigor of time more successfully than many others, are the small cards that were distributed with cigarettes; however even these are not plentiful and some time may be involved in finding the early ones showing uniforms. Probably the most sought after cigarette cards are the military ones issued by Kinney, who made Sweet Caporal cigarettes along with other popular tobacco products. This series shows over five hundred and fifty types of uniforms, beside military medals, foreign arms, state seals and ancient war ships. They are of particular value to the military collector and historian because, besides uniforms of the regulars, there are a great many showing the volunteer uniforms mentioned earlier.

Cards were made and distributed all over the world, with each country showing not only pictures featuring their own nation but those of other nations as well. Mass distribution of cigarette cards in the United States slowed down after the turn of the century, but there were still a few experimental issues made as late as the 1930's by Herbert Tareyton, Lucky Strike, Pall Mall and others. Distribution in other countries continued strongly throughout the first half of the twentieth century and was discontinued only during paper shortages of World Wars I and II. Collecting cigarette cards is a hobby in itself, just as coin and stamp collecting, and this accounts for the variety of asking prices when you buy them; there are rare ones and common ones. Early ones on popular subjects such as sports and uniforms are naturally rare and many times in poor condition when found — in the nineteenth century a favorite way to spend the evening was looking at picture cards. Being pasted in albums, fingered, torn out to trade and eventually stored in a damp basement, shed, or sun-baked attic made casualties not only of cards but of other historic papers and journals that are eagerly sought today for research.

Picture cards were so much in demand that album cards were made and sold, and naturally there were many colored postcards which included military subjects. Many postcards are still made that have excellent information on military uniforms. In the United States, museums and art galleries publish the majority, while other countries turn out many for distribution through regular trade channels and through museums.

Almost inevitably at sometime during service, be they enlisted men or officers, soldiers have an inspiration to write a book telling of their adventures, extolling their military knowledge, or exposing the Army. Naturally, in most cases this inspiration passes, but still many have put their views on paper and eventually see them in print. Needless to say, many who wrote should have let the inspiration pass, but by the same token some have produced very creditable manuscripts that add greatly to man's storehouse of knowledge. With the progress of printing in the nineteenth century, the flow of military

lored post cards having their origin in a variety of countries of the world are now distributed by
ny museums, art galleries, stationery stores and dealers in military miniatures. Those showing
forms, frequently carry valuable descriptive material on the back. Cards from an earlier period
sometimes found in antique and second-hand book shops.

histories increased. More and more military histories continue at present to come off the presses, and even some of the earlier works that have not survived time physically are being reprinted. These works, combined with those of professional historians and military observers, as well as periodicals and newspapers, can furnish a bonanza of information for the student if he studies and cross-examines the various accounts, paying close attention to all footnotes and references. Just as the Apostles saw and recorded the same events differently, so historians and observers each see the same thing many times from different angles.

The military miniature diorama maker should also keep in mind conditions and circumstances existing at the time of the event he is depicting. It is important, too, to keep in mind the desire of the soldier to be as comfortable as possible on the line and in forward areas. From the time before Caesar's legions, through the wars of history, including the World Wars, soldiers have utilized clothing, weapons and equipment of the enemy and of civilians, sometimes through necessity and sometimes for comfort and efficiency. Therefore, even though the student may have at hand complete dress regulations as set forth by any particular government for its soldiers, he should allow for existing conditions when clothing his miniatures.

One of the first things a collector of military miniatures should do is start a "morgue". This is a term used by professional artists to describe their files of reference pictures and notes. No matter how the morgue is housed, whether in notebooks, boxes, or filing cabinets, it should be separated into period and nationality: include with an index so that material can be found quickly. Beside cards, prints, notes and sketches, magazines published today offer many accurate colored pictures of soldiers and battle scenes in both advertising and in articles; these too should be clipped and added to the morgue.

All of the foregoing is just an idea of the many ways information can be obtained, depending entirely on your own ingenuity and interest in the subject. Once the search is started, one source will lead to another and the time spent will offer just as much entertainment as the final construction of the diorama or figure.